P9-CLA-064

Instant Immersion

German™

developed by Mary March, M.A.

written by Eva-Maria Barthel, Ph.D.

© 2008 Topics Entertainment, Inc.

3401 Lind Ave. S.W. Renton, WA 98057 U.S.A.

www.InstantImmersion.com

All rights reserved. No part of this book may be reproduced or transmitted in any form or by any means, electronic or mechanical, including photocopying without permission in writing from the Publisher.

Instant Immersion™

developed by Mary March, M.A.
written by Eva-Maria Barthel, Ph.D.

Edited by Laura Wideburg, Ph.D.
Illustrations by Elizabeth Haidle
Art Director: Paul Haidle
Design by Paul Haidle
Maps by Lonely Planet®

Printed on 100% recycled paper. Printed in the U.S.A.

TABLE OF CONTENTS

Bonus! Portable Video Phrase Book DVD

INTRODUCTION

Willkommen to *Instant Immersion German™!* An understanding of other cultures is critical in becoming part of a larger global community. Knowing how to communicate in other languages is one way to facilitate this process. You have chosen a truly global language to learn. There are diverse German cultures in Germany, Switzerland, and Austria having a worldwide influence on politics, manufacturing, the high-tech industry, literature, philosophy, the arts and music.

Now let's get down to learning some German. Did you know that a large part of the English vocabulary is similar to the German language? This means you already know the meaning of many German words such as: *schwimmen* (to swim), *waschen* (to wash), *der Arme* (arm). Other German words look very much like their English equivalents: *das Radio, die Banane, das Auto, die Musik* are just a few. You just have to learn the pronunciation. (And you will see that learning German pronunciation is not as difficult as you might think!)

This book will help you learn the basics of communicating in German in a way that will be fun and easy for you. We include many popular phrases and expressions and show you how these are used in real life through example conversations and stories. Our book also provides an easy pronunciation system that will give you the confidence you need to speak German. A wide range of interesting and valuable topics give you a firm grounding in the language, including how to order food like a local, how to travel comfortably within the country, even what to do when things go 'wrong'.

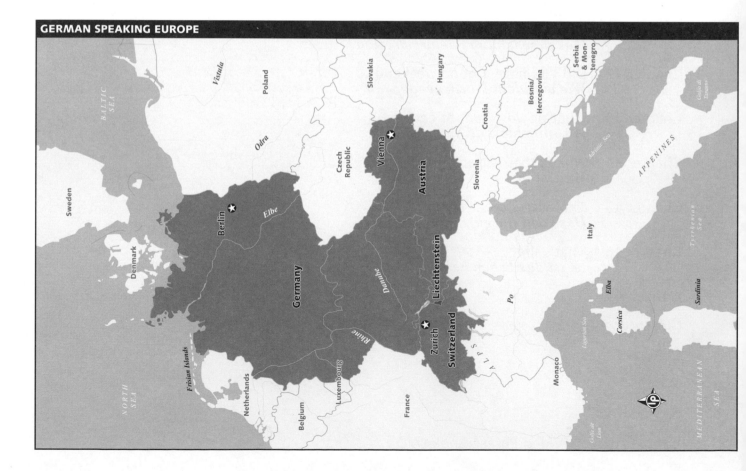

GERMAN SPEAKING EUROPE

PRONUNCIATION GUIDE

The pronunciation of German is very consistent. Vowels and consonants are pronounced in the same way no matter how they appear in each word. While English and German share many pronunciation rules, particularly with respect to consonants, differences do occur. The following chart serves as a guideline when practicing proper pronunciation in German.

German vowels and consonants	approximate equivalent in English	notation in the pronunciation key
a	long as in bar	aa
	short as in pasta	ah
ä	bad	a
e	short as in bed	e
e; ee	[no direct English equivalent] prolonged e as in buffet or the French café	é
i	short as in is	i
e; i; ie	long as in bee or believe	ee
o	long as in nose [where "o" is pronounced longer and lips are rounded]	O
	short as in not	o'
ö	word	o
u	long as in you or loose	oo
	short as in book	u'
ü	[no English equivalent; first pronounce the German u, then, with your tongue and mouth remaining in the same position, pronounce the short German i]	ü
ei; ai	eye	ay
au	ouch	ou
äu; eu	boy	oy
j	yacht	Y
g	good	g
z	pizza	ts
s; ß	sun, zebra	s,z
ch	[no English equivalent; pronounce as "k" but instead of opening the back of your throat, blow air through it]	CH
sch	shine	SCH
st	mostly pronounced as German sch + t	SCHt
sp	mostly pronounced as German sch + p	SCHp
v	fish	f
w	generally pronounced as "v", as in vote	v

This book has 16 chapters. You can work through the book chapter by chapter or skip around to the topics that most interest you. Study the expressions and vocabulary before reading the dialog or story. Say them out loud to practice your pronunciation. Read through the dialog or story as many times as you need in order to understand it. Then read it out loud. Check your answers to the exercises in the Answer Key in the back of the book. Finally, get in a German mood! Have a *Bratwurst,* hike in the mountains with some *Wanderlust,* listen to some Beethoven, or snuggle up at home with some *Glühwein* (hot spiced wine) in an atmosphere of *Gemütlichkeit.* But have fun learning German!

CHAPTER 1

(gooten mo'rgen)
Guten morgen!
Good morning!

(es ist meer egaal)
Es ist mir egal.
I don't care.

(es muCHt meer niCHts ous)
Es macht mir nichts aus.
It's all the same to me.

(lahs u'ns gé-en)
Lass uns gehen.
Let's go.

VOCABULARY

(er)
er
he

(der mahn)
der Mann
man

(der mo'rgen)
der Morgen
morning

(zee)
sie
she

(dee frou)
die Frau
woman

(SCHpreCHen)
sprechen
to speak

(gooten mo'rgen)
Guten Morgen!
Good morning!

(vee gét es deer)
Wie geht es dir?
How are you?

(es gét meer goot)
Es geht mir gut.
I'm fine.

(doo)
du
you

(vo'len)
wollen
want

(moCHten)
möchten
would like

(némen)
nehmen
to take

(haaben)
haben
to have

(géen)
gehen
to go

(dahs aabentessen)
das Abendessen
dinner

(esen)
essen
to eat

(dahs mitahkesen)
das Mittagessen
lunch

(der mo'rgen)
der Morgen
morning

(dahs brotCHen)
das Brötchen
breakfast roll

(dahs frühSCHtük)
das Frühstück
breakfast

(frühSCHtüken)
frühstücken
to have breakfast

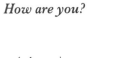

DIALOG

Es ist Morgen.

(mitayn ahnder)

Eine Frau und ein Mann–Sabine und Klaus–sprechen miteinander.

to each other

Sabine: Guten Morgen, Klaus. Wie geht es dir?

Klaus: Guten Morgen, Sabine. Es geht mir gut. Und dir?

Sabine: Es geht mir gut. Wo möchtest du frühstücken?

(weer konen tsoo dem kafé im)

Klaus: Es ist mir egal. Wir können zu dem Café

(hOtel gé-en)

im Hotel gehen. Ich möchte ein Brötchen essen.

(iCH ouch)

Sabine: Ich auch! Lass uns gehen!

PRACTICE

frühstücken	Abendessen	möchten	nehmen
Mittagessen	wo	du	Brötchen

Fill in the blanks using the words in the box.

1. Klaus geht zum _____ .

2. Wo möchtest _____ ?

3. Zum _____ möchte Sabine

   ein _____ essen.

4. _____ möchtest du essen?

MATCHING

Match the sentence with the picture.

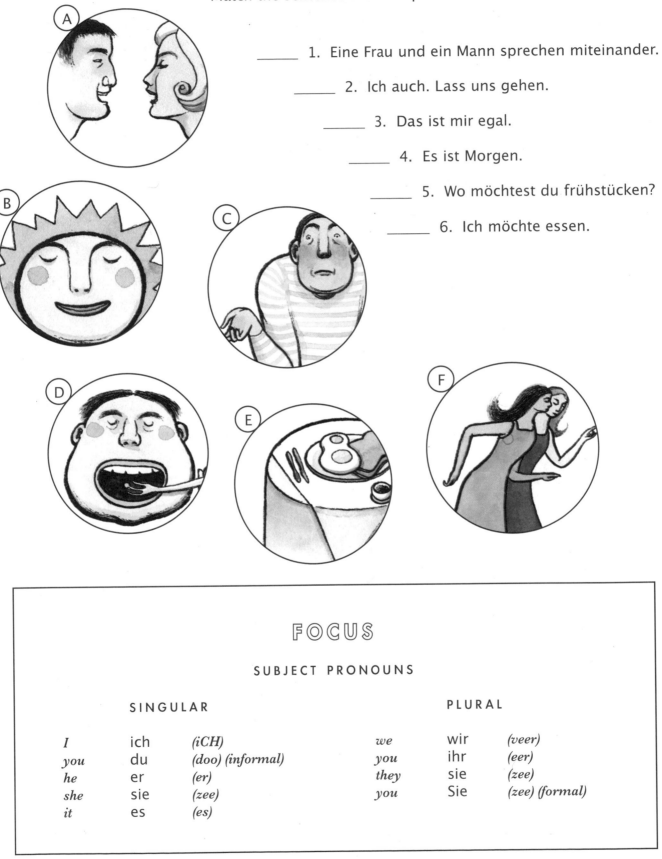

_____ 1. Eine Frau und ein Mann sprechen miteinander.

_____ 2. Ich auch. Lass uns gehen.

_____ 3. Das ist mir egal.

_____ 4. Es ist Morgen.

_____ 5. Wo möchtest du frühstücken?

_____ 6. Ich möchte essen.

FOCUS

SUBJECT PRONOUNS

SINGULAR			PLURAL		
_I_	ich	_(iCH)_	_we_	wir	_(veer)_
you	du	_(doo) (informal)_	_you_	ihr	_(eer)_
_he_	er	_(er)_	_they_	sie	_(zee)_
she	sie	_(zee)_	_you_	Sie	_(zee) (formal)_
_it_	es	_(es)_			

VERB CONJUGATIONS

(iCH ese etvahs)
Ich esse etwas.
a little

(essen)
essen
to eat

(veer esen feel)
Wir essen viel.
a lot

(doo ist flaySCH)
Du isst Fleisch.
meat

(eer est pahstah)
Ihr esst Pasta.
pasta

(zee ist im outo)
Sie isst im Auto.
car

(zee esen ahm SCHtrahnt)
Sie essen am Strand.
beach

(er ist ahm SCHtrahnt)
Er isst am Strand.
beach

(zee esen im bett)
Sie essen im Bett.
in bed

NOTES

The formal *"Sie"* (same as the third person plural, except capitalized) is used to address individuals and groups with whom the speaker is not acquainted or to whom the speaker has only established loose or superficial contact.

This includes, for the most part, hierarchical relationships such as superiors at the workplace or teachers in school. After you have familiarized yourself with the conjugation model below, return to the following examples and notice the different verb endings when using the formal *"Sie"* and the informal *"du"*.

FORMAL: Herr Schmidt, wo möcht<u>en</u> Sie essen? *Mr. Schmidt, where would you like to eat?*

Nehm<u>en</u> Sie das Buch herr Schmidt? *Mr. Schmidt, are you going to take the book?*

INFORMAL: Paul, wo möcht<u>est</u> du essen? *Paul, where would you like to eat?*

Nimm<u>st</u> du das Buch Paul? *Paul, are you going to take the book?*

NEHMEN
to take

ich nehme	*(iCH néme)*	I take
du nimmst	*(doo nimst)*	you take
er/sie/es nimmt	*(er, zee, es nimt)*	he, she, it takes
wir nehmen	*(veer némen)*	we take
ihr nehmt	*(eer némt)*	you take
sie/Sie nehmen	*(zee némen)*	they/you (formal) take

Here are some common expressions with *nehmen:*

Nimmst du ein Brötchen?
Are you having a roll?

Ich nehme den Zug.
I'm taking the train.

Nimm dich in Acht!
Watch out!

CHAPTER 2

(iCH haabe hu'nger)
Ich habe hunger!
I'm hungry!

Reading in German will help you learn how to understand the language. It is an easy, effective way to increase your vocabulary and knowledge of grammatical structures. Practice saying the idioms and vocabulary words. Study the meaning of each. Then read the story silently, trying to understand it. Read the story again out loud, focusing on the pronunciation of the words.

(vahs für ayn glük)
Was für ein Glück!
What luck!

(iCH hahbe hu'nger)
Ich habe Hunger!
I'm hungry!

VOCABULARY

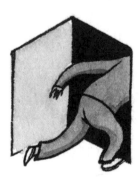

(betrit)
er betritt
(3rd p.singular)
he enters

(ferlast)
verlässt
(3rd p. singular)
leave

(glükliCH)
glücklich
happy

(trourig)
traurig
sad

(froyndinen)
Freundinnen
friends
(female form)

(kaze)
Käse
cheese

(gében)
geben
give

NUMBERS

If you want to understand a room number, tell someone your phone number, or understand how much something is you are considering buying, you need numbers. Try to memorize the numbers 0–10 now. (Practice counting throughout the day!) More numbers will be introduced in later chapters.

0	1	2	3	4	5
(nu'l)	*(ayns)*	*(tsvay)*	*(dray)*	*(feer)*	*(fünf)*
null	eins	zwei	drei	vier	fünf

6	7	8	9	10
(zeks)	*(zeeben)*	*(ahCHt)*	*(noyn)*	*(tsén)*
sechs	sieben	acht	neun	zehn

PRACTICE

Write the answers to these simple arithmetic problems in words.

1. drei + eins = _____

2. sechs + vier = _____

3. zwei + drei = _____

4. acht – fünf = _____

5. neun – acht = _____

6. zehn – drei = _____

7. vier x zwei = _____

8. drei x drei = _____

STORY

(eere) *(resto'rung)*
Anna und ihre Freundin Juliane sind in einem Restaurant.
her

Anna isst ein Käsebrötchen.

Juliane hat zwei Käsebrötchen.

Peter betritt das Restaurant.

(SCHtelt)
Anna stellt Peter Juliane vor.
introduce

(es froyt miCH, diCH kenen tsoo lernen) *(saakt)*
"Es freut mich, dich kennen zu lernen", sagt Peter.
I am delighted to meet you. *says*

(fraakt)
Dann fragt Anna Peter, ob er Hunger hat.
ask *if*

"Ja, ich habe Hunger", sagt er.

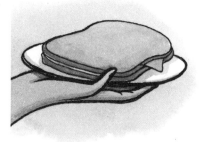

(eem)
Juliane gibt ihm ein Brötchen.
him

(erveedert)
"Danke, was für ein Glück", erwidert Peter. Er ist sehr glücklich.
respond

PRACTICE

The statements below are all false. Change each one to make it true.

1. Anna und ihre Freundin essen im Auto.

_____

2. Juliane hat drei Brötchen. _____

3. Peter verlässt das Restaurant. _____

4. Peter ist traurig. _____

VERB FOCUS

(sint)
Wir sind glücklich.
We are happy.

(bist)
Du bist glücklich.
You are happy.

(ist)
Sie ist glücklich.
She is happy.

(zint)
Sie sind glücklich.
They are happy.

(bin)
Ich bin traurig.
I am sad.

(zayt)
Ihr seid traurig.
You are sad.

(ist)
Er ist traurig.
He is sad.

Here are some useful sentences with the verb "be":

(zee ist arztin/lérerin/künstlerin)
Sie ist Ärztin/Lehrerin/Künstlerin.
She is a doctor/teacher/artist.

(mir ist SCHleCHt)
Mir ist schlecht.
I am feeling sick.

(weer sint SCHpat)
Wir sind spät.
We are late.

(vahs ist lOs)
Was ist los?
What's the matter?

(zee sint in aynem konzért)
Sie sind in einem Konzert.
They are at a concert.

CHAPTER 3

(entSCHu'ldigu'ng)
Entschuldigung!
Excuse me!

If you are traveling to a foreign country, there will be many opportunities for you to start a conversation with native speakers of the language. Don't be shy! Of course some people will be in a hurry or won't want to talk to you. However, many people will be interested to meet someone traveling in their country. You'll want to learn some basic questions and appropriate responses as well as some useful expressions.

(iCH haabe doorst)
Ich habe Durst.
I'm thirsty.

(iCH bin müde)
Ich bin müde.
I'm tired.

(es mahCHt niCHts)
Es macht nichts.
Don't worry about it.

(es ist niCHt so' SCHlim)
Es ist nicht so schlimm.
It's not serious.

VOCABULARY

(Yaa)
ja
yes

(ous/fo'n)
aus/von
from

(vO)
wo
where

(ko'men)
kommen
come

(dee feraynigten SCHtaaten)
die Vereinigten Staaten
the United States

(SCHpreCHen)
sprechen
speak

(heer ist)
hier ist
here is

(iCH hayse)
ich heiße
my name is

(ayn vénig)
ein wenig
a little

(zOn)
der Sohn
son

(u'nt)
und
and

USEFUL EXPRESSIONS

Here are some ways to say yes and no:

(Yaa)
JA!
yes!

(nayn)
NEIN!
no!

(siCHer)
Sicher!
Certainly!

(nutürliCH niCHt)
Natürlich nicht!
Of course not!

(nutürliCH)
Natürlich!
Sure! Of course!

(im gégentayl)
Im Gegenteil!
On the contrary!

Sometimes bumping into people by accident can lead to introductions and even friendships. Read what Dan and Sylvie have to say to each other after they bump into each other in a doorway.

Dan Duncan: man   *Sylvie Bauer: woman*   *Anke: girl*   *David: boy*

1️⃣ **Dan:** Entschuldigung!

Sylvie: Es ist nicht so schlimm.

2️⃣ **Dan:** *(doytSCHe)* Sind Sie Deutsche?
German

Sylvie: *(vOher)* Ja, woher kommen Sie?
where from

3️⃣ **Dan:** Ich komme aus Seattle.
Ich heiße Dan Duncan.
Und Sie? Wie heißen Sie?

Sylvie: Ich heiße Sylvie Bauer.
(to'CHter) Das ist meine Tochter, Anke.
daughter

4️⃣ **Dan:** Hallo, Anke.
(ahlt) Wie alt bist du?

Anke: Ich bin acht Jahre alt.

5️⃣ **Dan:** *(sOn)* Das ist mein Sohn David.
son Er spricht ein wenig Deutsch.

Sylvie: Hallo, David. Wie alt bist du?

6️⃣ **David:** Ich bin fünf und ich habe
Hunger und ich habe
Durst und ich bin müde.

PRACTICE

Study the dialog. Then, see if you can write the missing question. The response is given.

1. _____ ? Ich bin zehn Jahre alt.

2. _____ ? Ich komme aus Seattle.

3. _____ ? Ich heiße Anke.

4. _____ ? Ich heiße Sylvia Bauer.

ASKING QUESTIONS IN GERMAN

A.   The easiest way to ask a question in German is to simply raise your voice at the end of a sentence.

Sie sind aus Deutschland?

Du hast Hunger?

B.   Put the noun or pronoun after the verb.

Kommst du aus Deutschland?   Hast du Hunger?   Heißt sie Schmidt?

C.   Still another way is to put an interrogative, or question word, at the beginning of the sentence.

Wie alt bist du?   Woher kommen Sie?   Wie heißt du?
How old are you?   *Where are you from?*   *What's your name?*

PRACTICE

Now practice asking questions. Write a question using the method indicated (A, B, or C), putting the words in the correct order.

Ex: Englisch/sprichst/du   (B) Sprichst du Englisch?

1. wie/du/heißt   (C) _____ ?

2. hast/du/Hunger   (A) _____ ?

3. hast/Hunger/du   (B) _____ ?

4. kommst/woher/du   (C) _____ ?

5. du/isst/Pizza   (B) _____ ?

6. du/alt/wie/bist   (C) _____ ?

VERB CONJUGATIONS

> *(haaben)*
> ## HABEN
> *to have*
>
> | | | |
> |---|---|---|
> | ich habe | *(iCH haabe)* | *I have* |
> | du hast | *(doo hahst)* | *you have* |
> | er/sie/es hat | *(er, zee, es haht)* | *he/she/one/it has* |
> | wir haben | *(veer haaben)* | *we have* |
> | ihr habt | *(eer hahpt)* | *you have* |
> | sie/Sie haben | *(zee haaben)* | *they/you (formal) have* |

Notice that some expressions in German with *haben* + noun are expressed in English with to be + adjective:

I am thirsty.	Ich habe Durst.	***I have thirst.***
I am hungry.	Ich habe Hunger.	***I have hunger.***

Here are some other useful expressions with the verb "have":

Er hat heute Geburtstag.
It's his birthday today.

Du hast Glück.
You're lucky.

Sie hat gute/schlechte Laune.
She is in a good/bad mood.

Du hast Recht.
You're right.

Ich habe Angst.
I'm afraid.

Es hat keinen Sinn.
There is no point in that.

> ## SPRECHEN
> *to speak*
>
> | | | |
> |---|---|---|
> | ich spreche | *(iCH SCHpreCHe)* | *I speak* |
> | du sprichst | *(doo SCHpriCHst)* | *you speak* |
> | er/sie/es spricht | *(er, zee, es SCHpriCHt)* | *he/she/one speaks* |
> | wir sprechen | *(veer SCHpreCHen)* | *we speak* |
> | ihr sprecht | *(eer SCHpreCHt)* | *you speak* |
> | sie/Sie sprechen | *(zee SCHpreCHen)* | *they/you (formal) speak* |

CHAPTER 4

(vee feel ko'stet dus)
Wie viel kostet das?
How much is it?

VOCABULARY

(vahs)
Was?
What?

(lahngsahm)
langsam
slowly

(aaber)
aber
but

(bite SCHon)
Bitte schön!
There you are. (or)
You are welcome.

VERBS

(ferSCHtéhen)
verstehen
understand

(moCHten)
möchten
would like

NOTE: When addressing people with their title (Mr, Mrs, Miss) use either *"Frau"* or *"Herr"* as in *"Danke, Herr Schmidt."* or *"Auf Wiedersehen, Frau Keller."* Unlike in English, titles always require that you mention a person's last name. For example, there is no German equivalent of the English "Yes, Sir."

Important note: The German equivalent of "Miss" is *"Frau"* and not *"Fräulein"*. Addressing women as *"Fräulein"* is considered outdated and sometimes even disrespectful.

(bittah)
Bitte.
Please.

(feelen dahnk)
Vielen Dank.
Thank you very much.

(bite)
Bitte.
You're welcome.

(ouf veedersén)
Auf Wiedersehen!
Good bye!

(nayn dahnke)
Nein, danke.
No, thank you.

(dahnke gern)
Danke, gern!
Yes, please.

NOTE: There are two ways to form negatives in German depending on whether you are negating a sentence or a noun. Nouns are negated with *"kein"*, sentences are negated with *"nicht"*. Compare the following examples.

(kaynen)
Ich habe keinen Hunger.
I am not hungry.

(niCHt)
Peter ist nicht glücklich.
Peter is not happy.

Er hat kein Auto.
He doesn't have a car.

Sie kommt nicht aus Seattle.
She is not from Seattle.

STORY

Es ist zehn Uhr morgens. Brigitte
und John sind in Hamburg. Brigitte
ist Deutsche. John ist Amerikaner,
aber er spricht ein wenig Deutsch.

(bakeray)
Sie sind in einer Bäckerei.
bakery

Angestellte: Guten Morgen.
(clerk)

Brigitte: Guten Morgen.

John: Guten Morgen.

Angestellte: Was möchten Sie?

(brOt)
Brigitte: Ich möchte ein Brot, bitte.
a loaf of bread

Angestellte: Und Sie? Was möchten Sie?

John: Ich verstehe Sie nicht.
          Sprechen Sie bitte langsam.

Angestellte: In Ordnung. Was möchten Sie?

(brotCHen)
John: Ich möchte zwei Brötchen, bitte.
rolls

Angestellte: Bitte schön.

Brigitte: *(mineraalvahser)*
Haben Sie Mineralwasser?

Angestellte: Natürlich. Bitte schön.

Brigitte: Vielen Dank. Wie viel kostet das?

Angestellte: Drei Euro, bitte.

Brigitte: Hier sind drei Euro.

Angestellte: Vielen Dank.

John und Brigitte: Auf Wiedersehen.

Angestellte: Auf Wiedersehen.

DO YOU UNDERSTAND?

Read the dialog carefully and see if you can answer these questions.
Check your answers in the back of the book.

1. Who is Deutsche in this dialog? _____

2. Why doesn't John understand? _____

3. What does John want to buy? _____

4. Who asks for mineral water? _____

5. Where does this scene take place? _____

ZAHLEN 11 - 21

11	12	13	14	15	16
(elf)	*(tsvolf)*	*(drayzén)*	*(firzén)*	*(fünfzén)*	*(seCHzén)*
elf	zwölf	dreizehn	vierzehn	fünfzehn	sechzehn

17	18	19	20	21
(zeepzén)	*(ahCHtzén)*	*(noynzén)*	*(tsvahnzig)*	*(aynoonttsvahntsiCH)*
siebzehn	achtzehn	neunzehn	zwanzig	einundzwanzig

WHAT WOULD YOU LIKE?

Was möchten Sie?
What would you like?

NOTE: "I would like" is the polite-conditional form of the verb "to want" and is commonly used, but it's always good to say "please" – at the beginning or end of the sentence-too.

(mogen)
MÖGEN
to like

ich mag	*(iCH maak)*	*I like*
du magst	*(doo maakst)*	*you like*
er, sie, es mag	*(er, zee, es maak)*	*he, she, it likes*
wir mögen	*(veer mogen)*	*we like*
ihr mögt	*(eer mokt)*	*you like*
sie mögen	*(zee mogen)*	*they like*
Sie mögen	*(zee mogen)*	*you like (formal)*

In the following exercise, write the numbers in words, just for practice. Review numbers 1–10 in Chapter 2 if you need to. Say the numbers out loud as you write them. Then, practice saying each sentence with *"bitte"* at the end.

For example: "Ich möchte ein Brötchen, bitte."

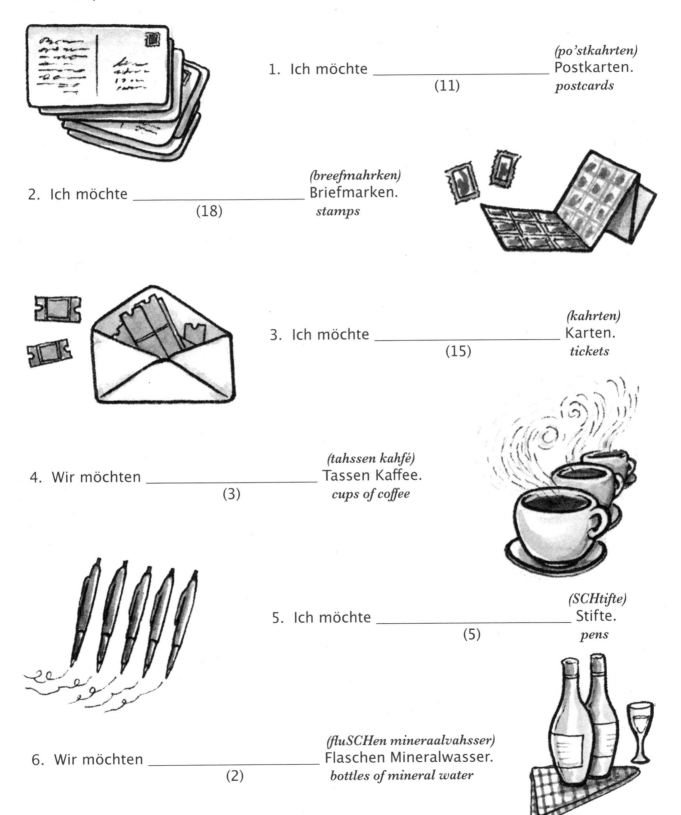

1. Ich möchte _____ Postkarten. *(po'stkahrten)* Postkarten. *postcards*
   (11)

2. Ich möchte _____ Briefmarken. *(breefmahrken)* Briefmarken. *stamps*
   (18)

3. Ich möchte _____ Karten. *(kahrten)* Karten. *tickets*
   (15)

4. Wir möchten _____ Tassen Kaffee. *(tahssen kahfé)* Tassen Kaffee. *cups of coffee*
   (3)

5. Ich möchte _____ Stifte. *(SCHtifte)* Stifte. *pens*
   (5)

6. Wir möchten _____ Flaschen Mineralwasser. *(fluSCHen mineraalvahsser)* Flaschen Mineralwasser. *bottles of mineral water*
   (2)

(velCHer taak ist hoyte)
Welcher Tag ist heute?
What day is it?

(es ist mir lahngvayliCH)
Es ist mir langweilig.
I am bored.

(argerliCH verden)
argerlich werden
to get angry

VOCABULARY

(geSCHaftsfrou)
die Geschäftsfrau
business woman

(lu'stig)
lustig
funny

(der prOgrumeerer)
der Programmierer
computer programmer

(hous)
das Haus
house

(outO)
das Auto
car

(net)
nett
nice

(dee ougen)
die Augen
eyes

(dee ahrbayt)
die Arbeit
work

(der SCHtern)
der Stern
star

FOCUS : VERBS

Most commonly, verbs describe the action that is carried out by the subject of a sentence. Subject and verb have to agree. This means that the correct ending has to be added to the end of the verb depending on whether the subject is I, you, he, she, a car, several cars etc. In proper grammatical terminology this is called a conjugation. English has dropped most of its verb endings and only conjugates the third person singular (he, she, it) as in he/she speaks, he/she likes, or in special verbs like "to be", where irregularities occur. In German, all the different personal pronouns (I, you, he, she, it etc.) have distinct endings. So far you have learned the endings for the present tense forms. All tenses (past, future, perfect, past perfect etc.) have their unique forms.

When verbs appear in a non-conjugated form they are called infinitives. In English, for example, I am, you are, he/she/it is etc. are all conjugated forms of the infinitive to be. In German, the infinitive is usually marked by an en-ending at the end of the verb as in *sprechen, möchten, wohnen.* The infinitive serves many different functions and is used to form some of the tenses. It is also the form of the verb that appears in a dictionary.

As in most languages, verbs are generally divided into regular and irregular verbs. This distinction is based on the modifications that occur when verbs appear in the different tenses. While some verbs simply add a particular set of endings and are entirely predictable, others undergo unexpected changes. In English, for example, the past tense form of the verb "to go" is went. This is a modification that cannot be derived from the verb by means of some sort of rule. The same holds true for German. Irregular verbs (also called strong verbs) and their specific changes have to be memorized. Most dictionaries include a list of the most common irregular verbs.

Some verbs undergo a vowel change in the second and third person singular (*du* and *er/ sie/es*). In Chapter 1 you might have noticed that the verb *nehmen* changes to *du nimmst* and *er/sie/es nimmt.* Another verb that follows this rule is *essen,* which changes to *du isst* and *er/sie/es isst* and *sprechen,* which changes to *du sprichst* and *er/sie/es spricht.* A good dictionary will tell you if such a vowel change occurs, usually by listing the third person singular.

One of the peculiarities of German is that some verbs are separable. In English many different meanings can be derived from one verb by adding prepositions to the verb as in to take up, to take on, to take off etc. In German, these prepositions do not only precede the verb but are actually merged into one word. Depending on the type of sentence as well as the tense, these verbs will sometimes appear in their merged form and sometimes in their separated form. For example, the German meaning of the English verb to arrive is *ankommen.* However, when you want to say *The train arrives on Monday* you have to say *Der Zug kommt am Montag an.* The preposition has been separated and moved to the end of the sentence.

With different endings, vowel changes, irregular forms and separable particles, verbs appear to be a very difficult topic in German. In many respects, however, German is less complex than English. The English forms I live, I have lived, I have been living all translate into the one simple form *ich wohne.* German does not differentiate between certain aspects of expressing temporal relations. In fact, in colloquial language, familiarity with the present tense form of verbs and one past tense form usually suffices to communicate in German.

Jan und Monika wohnen *(vOnen)*
live

in einem großen blauen

und rosa Haus.

Sie haben einen kleinen

Garten mit roten und

(bloomen)
gelben Blumen.
flowers

Jan ist Computerprogrammierer.

Er ist 25 Jahre alt und hat grüne

Augen.

Im Allgemeinen ist er sehr nett,

(mahnCHmaal)
aber manchmal wird er ärgerlich.
sometimes

Jan mag seine Arbeit nicht. Es ist

ihm langweilig.

Monika ist Geschäftsfrau. Sie

ist 26 Jahre alt und hat braune

(bayde)
Augen. Sie ist lustig. Für beide
both
war es Liebe auf den ersten

Blick. Monikas Arbeit ist sehr
(interesahnt)
interessant. Ihre Arbeit gefällt ihr

sehr.

(beSCHaftigt)
Beide sind sehr beschäftigt.
busy

Jeden Montag fährt Monika mit dem Zug nach Stuttgart.

Jeden Mittwoch fährt Jan mit dem Auto nach Freiburg.

(tsoosahmen)
Aber jeden Freitag essen sie zusammen in einem Restaurant.
together

Das Restaurant heißt "Der Rote Stern".

PRACTICE

Complete the following sentences. Use the vocabulary and the dialog to help you.

1. Jan und Monika wohnen in einem großen blauen und rosa _____ .

2. Jan ist 25 _____ .

3. Im Allgemeinen ist Jan sehr _____ .

4. Monika ist _____ .

5. Jan gefällt seine _____ nicht.

6. Monika fährt mit dem _____ nach Stuttgart.

7. Jan fährt mit dem _____ nach Freiburg.

(vays)
weiß

(blou)
blau

(grou)
grau

(broun)
braun

(SCHvahrz)
schwarz

(orahnSCH)
orange

(gelp)
gelb

(grün)
grün

(rOsa)
rosa

(rOt)
rot

PRACTICE

(faarben)
die Farben
colors

See how many colors you can remember.
Fill in the crossword puzzle with German words.

ACROSS

1. yellow
2. gray
3. brown
4. orange

DOWN

2. green
5. red
6. pink
7. white
8. blue

DAYS OF THE WEEK

(mOntak)	*(deenstak)*	*(mitvo'CH)*	*(do'nerstak)*	*(fraytak)*	*(sahmstak)*	*(so'ntak)*
Montag	Dienstag	Mittwoch	Donnerstag	Freitag	Samstag	Sonntag
Monday	*Tuesday*	*Wednesday*	*Thursday*	*Friday*	*Saturday*	*Sunday*

Find the days of the week hidden in the puzzle. Then circle them.

u	a	c	s	a	m	s	t	a	g
m	i	t	t	w	o	c	h	s	o
i	d	d	i	e	n	s	t	a	g
v	f	r	e	i	t	a	g	m	t
s	o	n	n	t	a	g	e	e	t
q	c	s	c	m	g	u	a	d	i
d	o	n	n	e	r	s	t	a	g

PRACTICE

Put the *Tage* of the week in their correct order by putting
a number from 1 to 7 in front of each day.

_____ Mittwoch   _____ Sonntag   _____ Dienstag   _____ Freitag

_____ Montag   _____ Samstag   _____ Donnerstag

CHAPTER 6

(ist es vayt)
Ist es weit?
Is it far?

Understanding directions in another language is particularly difficult, but not impossible! Of course it helps to have a map *(Karte)* so you can look at the names of the streets as the person you ask points to them. You don't have to understand every word *(Wort)*.

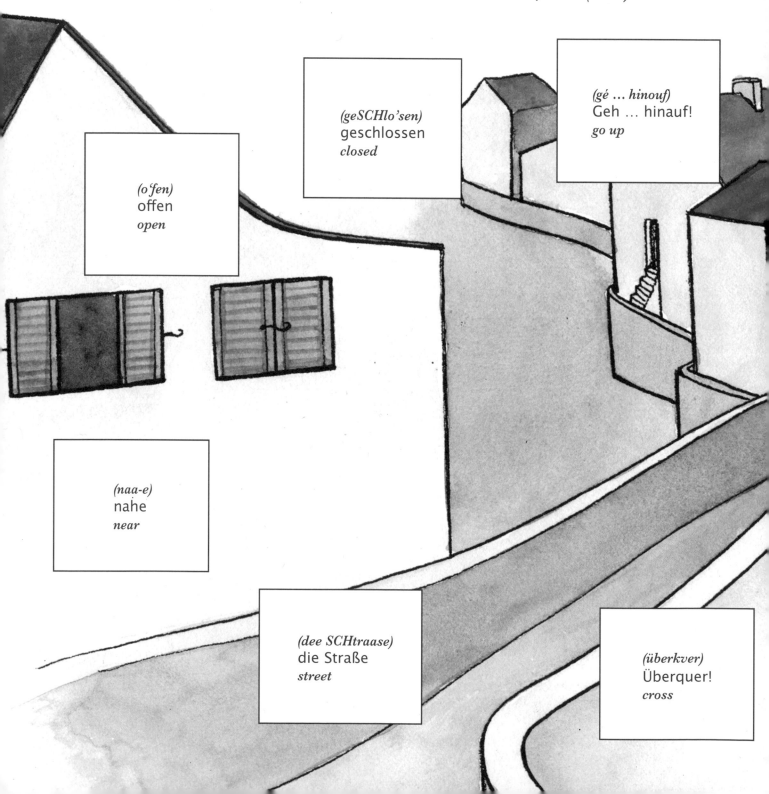

(geSCHlo'sen)
geschlossen
closed

(gé … hinouf)
Geh … hinauf!
go up

(o'fen)
offen
open

(naa-e)
nahe
near

(dee SCHtraase)
die Straße
street

(überkver)
Überquer!
cross

LISTEN FOR THE VERB.
This will generally be the first word you hear because it will be in the command form: Walk, Take, Go, Turn, Go up, Go down, Cross.

LISTEN FOR THE DIRECTION WORDS.
Right, left, straight ahead, next to, on the other side of, facing

LISTEN FOR THE NAMES OF THE STREETS.
These will be the hardest to understand. You can learn verbs and directions in advance, but names of people and places are more difficult because of the difference in pronunciation between English and German.

(vayt vek)
weit (weg)
far

(beeg ... up)
Bieg ...ab!
turn

(dee brüke)
die Brücke
bridge

(gé ... hinu'nter)
Geh ... hinunter!
go down

DIRECTIONS

The following forms are imperative (or command) forms for the informal address. The form is derived from the second person singular of the present tense and simply drops the ending. *Du gehst* becomes *Geh!* (Go!) *Du nimmst* becomes *Nimm!* (Take!) Note that the imperative retains the vowel change that occurs in the conjugation of the verb *nehmen*. Verbal particles and separable prepositions as in *hinuntergehen* are moved to the end of the imperative sentence: *Geh die Straße hinunter!* (Go down the street).

(ouf der ahnderen sayte)
auf der anderen Seite
on the other side (of)

(nében)
neben
next to

(gegenüber)
gegenüber
facing

(nahCH links)
nach links
to the left

(geradeous)
geradeaus
straight ahead

(nahCH reCHts)
nach rechts
to the right

(géen)
GEHEN
to go

ich gehe	*(iCH gée)*	*I go*
du gehst	*(doo gést)*	*you go*
er/sie/es geht	*(er, zee, es gét)*	*he, she, one goes*
wir gehen	*(veer géen)*	*we go*
ihr geht	*(eer gét)*	*you go*
sie gehen	*(zee géen)*	*they go*
Sie gehen	*(zee géen)*	*you go (formal)*

ORDINAL NUMBERS

You will need to know ordinal numbers when someone gives you directions (telling you which street to turn on). These numbers also come in handy when you need to tell which street your hotel is on, or which floor you want to stop on in a department store.

Wer hat das Rennen gewonnen?
Who won the race?

Using the numbers on the right fill in the blanks to help the race announcer list the winner and the first nine runner-ups. Say each number as you write it.

A is _____	F is _____	der Neunte	der Siebte
B is _____	G is _____	der Vierte	der Achte
C is _____	H is _____	der Erste	der Zehnte
D is _____	I is _____	der Sechste	der Zweite
E is _____	J is _____	der Fünfte	der Dritte

DIALOG

Michael and Nicole are standing outside a hotel, talking.

Michael: *(vOhin)*
Wohin gehst du?
Where are you going?

Nicole: *(keenO)*
Ich gehe ins Kino.
I'm going to the cinema.

Michael: Aber heute ist Montag. Das Kino ist geschlossen.
But today is Monday. The cinema is closed.

Nicole: Ja, das stimmt. Wohin gehst du?
Yes, that's right. Where are you going?

(zooerst)   *(bahnk)* *(dahnaaCH)*

Michael: Zuerst gehe ich auf die Bank. Danach gehe ich in den Park und dann gehe ich
then

(koufhous)
im Kaufhaus einkaufen. Möchtest du mitkommen?
department store   *shopping*   *come along*

(gloube)
Nicole: Nein, danke. Heute möchte ich nicht einkaufen gehen. Ich glaube, ich möchte in
think

(moosé-u'm)
ein Museum gehen.

(SCHtaatsgahleree)
Michael: Du kannst in die Staatsgalerie gehen. Sie ist Montags geöffnet.

Nicole: Toll! Wo ist die Staatsgalerie? Ist sie weit weg?

(mahn brouCHt) *(u'ngefar)*   *(foos)*
Michael: Nein, sie ist nicht sehr weit weg. Man braucht ungefähr 25 Minuten zu Fuß.
one needs   *about*

Nicole: Oh, das ist aber weit … Aber das ist in Ordnung. Es ist ein schöner Tag. Ich

mache einen Spaziergang.
(aynfahCH)
Michael: Du hast Recht. Also … geh einfach geradeaus und dann in die erste Straße
simply
(SCHilerSCHtraase)
links. Das ist die Schillerstraße. Bleib auf der Schillerstraße, bis du zur

(fürstenahllé)
Fürstenallee kommst. Dann biegst du rechts ab.

Nicole: Links in die Schillerstraße, dann rechts auf die Fürstenallee.

Michael: Geh die Fürstenallee hinunter, bis du zur Brücke kommst. Überquer die Brücke

(so'fo'rt)
und bieg dann sofort links ab.
immediately

Nicole: OK. Nach der Brücke links.

Michael: Richtig. Du siehst das Museum auf der rechten Seite.

Nicole: Danke, Michael. Bis später!

(ho'fe)
Michael: Bis später! Ich hoffe, du hast einen guten Spaziergang.
hope

CHAPTER 7

(velCHe yaareszayt hahst doo leeber)
Welche Jahreszeit hast du lieber?
Which season do you prefer?

(mit ahnderen vo'rten)
mit anderen Worten
in other words

(iCH ouCH)
Ich auch!
Me too!

(mayner maynu'ng nahCH)
meiner Meinung nach
in my opinion

THE SEASONS OF THE YEAR

(dee yaarestsayten)
die Jahreszeiten
the seasons of the year

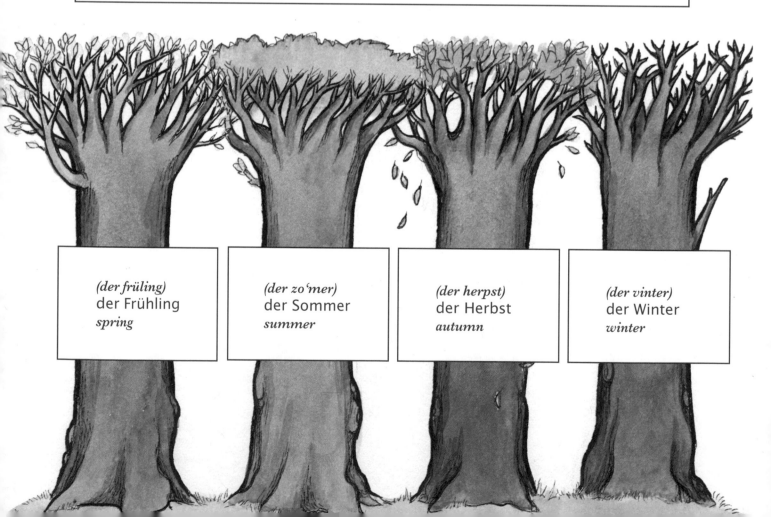

(der früling)
der Frühling
spring

(der zo'mer)
der Sommer
summer

(der herpst)
der Herbst
autumn

(der vinter)
der Winter
winter

THE MONTHS OF THE YEAR

(dee mOnahte des yaares)
die Monate des Jahres
the months of the year

(Yahnoo-ar)
Januar

(febroo-ar)
Februar

(marz)
März

(april)
April

(may)
Mai

(Yooni)
Juni

(Yooli)
Juli

(ougu'st)
August

(zeptember)
September

(oktOber)
Oktober

(november)
November

(detsember)
Dezember

STORY

Look at the pictures and read the sentences next to each one. See if you can figure out the meaning. Use the vocabulary and idioms on the previous pages to help you understand the story that follows the pictures.

(dee mu'ter)
die Mutter
mother

(der faater)
der Vater
father

(dee SCHvester)
die Schwester
sister

(der brooder)
der Bruder
brother

Die Mutter ist im Sommer am Strand.

1. _____

Der Vater ist im Winter in den Bergen.

2. _____

Der Bruder wandert im Herbst.

3. _____

Die Schwestern pflücken im Frühling die Blumen.

4. _____

Ich heiße Claudia Reich. Ich bin 20 Jahre alt. Ich habe eine sehr interessante Familie. Wir sind

(ferSCHeeden) *(féree-en)*
alle ganz verschieden. Wenn wir Ferien machen, möchte meine Mutter immer an den Strand
different *vacation*

gehen, aber mein Vater mag die Berge. Mit anderen Worten, meine Mutter möchte im Sommer

(leeber)
Ferien machen, aber mein Vater macht lieber im Winter Ferien. Er möchte im Dezember oder
rather

(loufen) *(vahlt)*
im Januar Ski laufen. Mein Bruder Uwe, der 17 Jahre alt ist, wandert gern im Wald. Er mag die

(deshahlb)
Farben des Herbstes wie orange, rot, gelb und braun. Deshalb macht er lieber im September
therefore

oder Oktober Ferien. Meine kleine Schwester Marion, die 15 Jahre alt ist, mag den Frühling.

(rayst)
Ich auch. Ich und Marion mögen all die schönen Blumen. Aber meine Schwester reist nicht
travel

gern. Meiner Meinung nach sind März, April und Mai die schönsten Monate zum Reisen.

Wann machen wir Ferien? Das ganze Jahr lang! Im September gehen wir jeden Samstag

wandern. Manchmal gehen wir auch im Winter und im Frühling wandern. An vielen

(vah'Chenenden)
Wochenenden im Dezember, Januar und Februar fahren wir Ski. Im Juni, Juli und August
weekends

(tsoo house)
gehen wir oft an den Strand. Oft bleiben wir auch zu Hause. Alle sind glücklich.
at home

PRACTICE

See if you can translate the following sentences into German.

1. My father prefers the winter.

_____

2. My brother, Uwe, who is 17, likes to hike in the forest.

_____

3. When do we take our vacation?

_____

4. From time to time we also go hiking in the winter and spring.

_____

5. I'm 20 years old.

_____

6. He likes the colors of autumn (orange, red, yellow, brown).

_____

7. Me too! Janine and I love the beautiful flowers.

_____

FOCUS

NOUN GENDER

All German nouns are either masculine, feminine, or neuter in gender. Sometimes it is easy to figure out which group a noun belongs to as in *der Amerikaner,* an American man, and *die Amerikanerin,* an American woman. Other times it just doesn't make any sense: *der Tisch* (the table) is masculine and *die Lampe* (the lamp) is feminine.

Try to learn the definite articles *(der, die, das)* together with the nouns:

> das Haus, die Blume, das Jahr, der Monat, die Familie, das Museum

This will help you remember the gender.

There are 3 different ways of
saying "the" (the definite article):

FEMININE

MASCULINE

MASCULINE: der Vater, der Strand, der Morgen, der Abend

FEMININE: die Mutter, die Schwester, die Straße, die Jahreszeit

NEUTER: das Kind, das Auto, das Jahr, das Haus

PLURAL: The plural form of the definite article is *die* for all nouns:
die Kinder, die Autos, die Straßen, die Jahreszeiten, die Häuser.

Choose the definite article that goes with these nouns.
You may have to look back at previous chapters!

1. _____ Schwester

2. _____ Strand

3. _____ Familie

4. _____ Käse

5. _____ Auto

6. _____ Mann

7. _____ Morgen

8. _____ Jahreszeit

9. _____ Museum

10. _____ Straße

There are 2 different ways of saying "a" (the indefinite article):
As in English there is no plural form of the indefinite article.

MASCULINE AND NEUTER: ein Auto, ein Mann, ein Kind, ein Vater

FEMININE: eine Mutter, eine Blume, eine Straße

CHAPTER 8

(dahs ist mayne fumeelee-e)
Das ist meine Familie.
This is my family.

There is a good chance that if you make a German friend *(Freund)*, you will be introduced to some of his or her family members at some point. Not only is it important to be able to understand these words that show family relationships, but it's also useful to be able to introduce and talk about the members of your family *(Familie)*. Say the words out loud.

(der hoot)
der Hut
hat

(grOs)
groß
tall

(klayn)
klein
little

(dee haare)
die Haare
hair

(lahng)
lang
long

(ku'rz)
kurz
short

(der é-e-mun)
der Ehemann
husband

dee é-e-frou
die Ehefrau
wife

FOCUS

THE FAMILY

MALE

der Vater	*(der faater)*	*father*
der Großvater	*(der grOsfaater)*	*grandfather*
der Schwiegervater	*(der SCHveegerfaater)*	*father-in-law*
der Bruder	*(der brooder)*	*brother*
der Sohn	*(der sOn)*	*son*
der Enkel	*(der enkel)*	*grandson*
der Onkel	*(der o'nkel)*	*uncle*
der Neffe	*(der nefe)*	*nephew*
der Ehemann	*(der é-e-mahn)*	*husband*
die Eltern	*(dee eltern)*	*parents*

FEMALE

die Mutter	*(dee mu'ter)*	*mother*
die Großmutter	*(dee grOsmu'ter)*	*grandmother*
die Schwiegermutter	*(dee SCHveegermu'ter)*	*mother-in-law*
die Schwester	*(dee SCHvester)*	*sister*
die Tochter	*(dee to'CHter)*	*daughter*
die Enkelin	*(dee enkelin)*	*granddaughter*
die Tante	*(dee tahnte)*	*aunt*
die Nichte	*(dee niCHte)*	*niece*
die Ehefrau	*(dee é-e-frou)*	*wife*
die Eltern	*(dee eltern)*	*parents*

STORY

(fahmeelee-e)
Peter hat eine kleine Familie. Seine Mutter heißt Gerda. Sie ist klein, hat graue Haare

(lébhahft)
und ist sehr lebhaft. Sein Vater heißt Siegfried. Er ist groß und er trägt gern Hüte. Peter
   dynamic   *wear*

hat keine Schwester, aber er hat einen Bruder, Bernd. Er mag Bernd sehr. Bernd ist sehr

(ferhayraatet)
lustig und er ist mit Kerstin verheiratet, Peters Schwägerin. Sie hat lange schwarze Haare,
   married

ist sehr schön und auch sehr nett. Sie haben keine Kinder. Peters Frau heißt Andrea. Sie ist

(inteligent)
klein, hat braune Haare und ist sehr intelligent. Peters Schwiegermutter heißt Elisabeth

und ihr Mann heißt Albert, Peters Schwiegervater. Peter und Andrea haben eine Tochter.

(leept)   *(beso'nders)*
Sie heißt Nicole. Sie ist 11 Jahre alt und liebt ihre Familie, besonders ihre Großeltern.
           love   *especially*

Nicole ist sehr lebhaft. Jeden Tag treibt sie Sport oder fährt mit dem Fahrrad. Und Peter?

(goot ousehend)
Er ist gut aussehend, aber nicht besonders intelligent.
good-looking

PRACTICE

Fill in the blanks under each picture.
  a) Write the name of the person.
  b) Write what relationship that person is to Peter. (Be sure to include the definite article *der, die, das* before the word.)

1. a _____
   b _____
2. a _____
   b _____

3. a _____
   b _____
4. a _____
   b _____

(Peter)

5. a _____
   b _____

6. a _____
   b _____
7. a _____
   b _____

8. a _____
   b _____

FOCUS

Now see if you can answer these questions. Check your answers in the back of the book.

1. Wer ist sehr intelligent? _____

2. Wer ist klein und hat graue Haare? _____

3. Wer ist mit Kerstin verheiratet? _____

4. Wer liebt die Großeltern? _____

5. Wer ist gut aussehend? _____

ADJECTIVES

When adjectives – such as *klein, kurz, schön, lang, lebhaft, rot, blau* etc. – precede nouns they have to be inflected, that is, endings have to be added to the adjectives. The proper adjective endings depend on a number of factors. For example, is the following noun feminine, masculine or neuter? Does the noun appear in its plural form? Does a definite article (or other modifying particle) precede adjective and noun? Does the noun take the position of the subject of the sentence (nominative), the direct object or the indirect object? While a detailed discussion of this topic is beyond the scope of this book, simply try to remember the following rules:

When a definite article precedes a noun in the nominative case, add –e to the adjective:

> die kleine Frau, der kleine Mann, das kleine Haus

When a definite article precedes nouns in their plural form, add –en to the adjective in all cases:

> die kleinen Frauen, die kleinen Männer, die kleinen Häuser

When there is no article preceding nouns in their plural form in the nominative case, add –e to the adjective:

> kleine Frauen, kleine Männer, kleine Häuser

Add the endings to the following adjectives. The first one is done for you.

1. die Frau *(groß)* _____die große Frau_____

2. die Männer *(plural)* *(klein)* _____

3. Töchter *(plural)* *(gut aussehend)* _____

4. der Hut *(klein)* _____

5. die Hüte *(plural)* *(blau)* _____

6. der Vater *(intelligent)* _____

FEMININE		MASCULINE
With feminine nouns		*With masculine and neuter nouns*
(mayne tahnte) meine Tante *my aunt*	**MY**	*(mayn o'nkel)* mein Onkel *my uncle*
(dayne tahnte) deine Tante *your aunt*	**YOUR**	*(dayn o'nkel)* dein Onkel *your uncle*
(eere tahnte) ihre Tante *her aunt*	**HER**	*(eer o'nkel)* ihr Onkel *her uncle*
(sayne tahnte) seine Tante *his aunt*	**HIS**	*(zayn o'nkel)* sein Onkel *his uncle*
(u'nsere tahnte) unsere Tante *our aunt*	**OUR**	*(u'nzer o'nkel)* unser Onkel *our uncle*
(oyre tahnte) eure Tante *your aunt*	*(plural)* **YOUR**	*(oyer o'nkel)* euer Onkel *your uncle*
(eere tahnte) ihre Tante *their aunt*	*(also used for formal address)* **THEIR**	*(eer o'nkel)* ihr Onkel *their uncle*

PRACTICE

Now see if you can put the appropriate possessive adjective in front of the following nouns:

1. _____ Familie
   my

2. _____ Haus
   his

3. _____ Vater
   her

4. _____ Schwester
   your (fam.)

5. _____ Brüder *(pl.)*
   their

6. _____ Hut
   your (formal)

7. _____ Freunde *(pl.)*
   my

8. _____ Mutter
   their

9. _____ Frau
   his

10. _____ Eltern *(pl.)*
    our

CHAPTER 9

(vee ist dahs vetter)
Wie ist das Wetter?
What's the weather?

Being able to chat about the weather *(das Wetter)* is a useful skill to have in another language. Whether you're at a bus stop, in a restaurant, or making small talk with a desk clerk at a hotel, the weather is a safe, popular topic (and often necessary if you're planning outdoor activities).

SIDEBAR: *Es ist kalt* means "It is cold". When you want to say "I am cold" you have to say *Mir ist kalt* or *Es ist mir kalt,* which literally means "It is cold to <u>me</u>, or, I am <u>feeling</u> cold". When you say *Ich bin kalt* you are describing yourself as a person with a cold personality!

WEATHER EXPRESSIONS

(hays)
Es ist heiß.
It's hot.

(kahlt)
Es ist kalt.
It's cold.

(vindiCH)
Es ist windig.
It's windy.

(regnet)
Es regnet.
It's raining.

(zo'nig)
Es ist sonnig
It's sunny.

(SCHon)
Es ist schön.
It's beautiful.

(fu'rCHtbaares veter)
Es ist ein furchtbares Wetter.
It's horrible weather.

(SCHnayt)
Es schneit.
It's snowing.

DIALOG

This is a telephone conversation between Liesel and her mother. Liesel is 22 years old and is living in Alaska for 1 year doing research as part of her university graduate studies. Her mother lives in Fulda.

Liesel: Hallo Mama.

Mutter: Hallo, mein Schatz. Wie geht es dir?

Liesel: Es geht mir gut.
Aber es ist mir kalt.

(aarmes)
Mutter: Mein armes Kind. Schneit es?

Liesel: Mama, es ist Winter und ich bin in Alaska.

Natürlich schneit es!

Wie ist das Wetter in Fulda?

Mutter: Heute regnet es viel, aber gestern

war es sonnig. Gestern war es sehr warm,

aber heute ist es kalt.

(veeder)
Morgen soll es wieder sonnig sein.
again

Wann kommst du nach Hause?

Liesel: Ich weiß nicht. Ich habe viel Arbeit. *(ahrbayt)*
work

Ich arbeite jeden Tag außer Sonntag. *(ouser)*
except

Mutter: Ach du meine Güte! Wo arbeitest du denn?

Ich fliege jeden Montag nach Nome und bleibe zwei *(fleege)* *(blaybe)*
fly *stay*

Tage. Oft fahre ich mit dem Auto nach Fairbanks.

Es ist weit weg! Ich arbeite lieber hier in Anchorage.

Am Freitag muss ich wieder nach Fairbanks. Wann

kommst du zu Besuch? *(besooCH)*
for a visit

Mutter: Ach, doch nicht jetzt! Nicht im Winter! Du weißt, ich mag den Schnee nicht. *(yezt)*
now

Ich möchte im Sommer nach Alaska kommen, wenn es warm ist.

Liesel: Na gut. Ja, es ist zu kalt hier im Winter.

Vielleicht komme ich in den Ferien nach Hause.

Mutter: Das ist eine gute Idee! Komm nach Hause, mein Schatz. *(eedé)*
idea

Du weißt, hier scheint manchmal die Sonne.

Und es gibt Schnee.

Liesel: OK, Mama. Bis bald.

Mutter: Auf Wiederhören, mein Schatz.

Kopf hoch!

PRACTICE

Verstehen Sie das?
Do you understand?

See if you can answer the following questions based on the dialog.

1. Who is cold? _____

2. Where is Liesel? _____

3. Where is it raining? _____

4. When does Liesel work? _____

5. When does her mom want to visit Alaska? _____

See if you can match each statement on the right to the appropriate picture of the person to make each statement true. Connect each of the circles with a line.

1. Sie möchte im Sommer nach Alaska kommen.

2. Sie arbeitet von Montag bis Samstag.

3. Sie fliegt im Dezember nach Hause

4. Sie fliegt manchmal mit dem Flugzeug zur Arbeit.

5. Sie arbeitet gern in Anchorage.

6. Sie sagt, sie mag keinen Schnee.

7. Sie sagt, es regnet.

8. Ihr ist kalt.

PRACTICE

Wie ist das Wetter?
What's the weather?

Let's see if you can complete the sentences with the weather expressions given. (You can peek back at Chapter 7 to review *Monate und Jahreszeiten*.)

1. _____ im Sommer.
                   it is hot

2. _____ im April.
                   it rains a lot

3. _____ im November.
                   it's bad weather

4. _____ im Januar.
                   it snows

5. _____ im Frühling.
                   it is windy

6. Heute _____.
                   it's beautiful

EXPRESSIONS FOR TIME

You may recall the words *"gestern"* (yesterday) and *"heute"* (today) from Chapter 6 when you learned about giving directions. Now let's add *"morgen"* (tomorrow) to your vocabulary. (Remember how *"Mutter"* described the weather in Fulda?)

(gestern)	*(hoyte)*	*(mo'rgen)*
gestern	heute	morgen

PRACTICE AND REVIEW

See if you can figure out which word doesn't belong in each of the series of words below. Write the words in the blanks.

_____ 1. heiß, Sommer, Sonne, Schnee

_____ 2. gestern, kalt, morgen, heute

_____ 3. viel, wann, wo, wer

_____ 4. arbeiten, besuchen, hier, gehen

_____ 5. Tag, Woche, Jahr, Frühling

MACHEN

(mahCHen)
to make/do

ich mache	*(iCH mahCHe)*	*I make*
du machst	*(doo mahCHst)*	*you make*
er/sie/es macht	*(er, zee, es mahCHt)*	*he, she, one makes*
wir machen	*(veer mahCHen)*	*we make*
ihr macht	*(eer mahCHt)*	*you make*
sie machen	*(zee mahCHen)*	*they make*
Sie machen (formal)	*(zee mahCHen)*	*you make*

KOMMEN

(ko'men)
to come

ich komme	*(iCH ko'me)*	*I come*
du kommst	*(doo ko'mst)*	*you come*
er/sie/es kommt	*(er, zee, es ko'mt)*	*he, she, one comes*
wir kommen	*(veer ko'men)*	*we come*
ihr kommt	*(eer ko'mt)*	*you come*
sie kommen	*(zee ko'men)*	*they come*
Sie kommen (formal)	*(zee ko'men)*	*you come*

(ko'm)	*(ko'men zee)*
Command: Komm! (informal)	Kommen Sie! (formal)

CHAPTER 10

(vee feel oor ist es)
Wie viel Uhr ist es?
Do you have the time?

You've learned the days of the week (Chapter 5) and the months of the year (Chapter 7). Now it's time to learn about how to tell time. If you need to, go back to Chapters 2 and 4 to review numbers up to 21. Later in this chapter you'll learn some more numbers that you'll need in order to say the minutes.

(goote loune haaben)
gute Laune haben
to be in a good mood

(vee bitte)
Wie bitte?
What?

(SCHleCHte loune haaben)
schlechte Laune haben
to be in a bad mood

(früh sayn)
früh sein
to be early

(mist)
Mist!
Darn!

(SCHpat sayn)
spät sein
to be late

VOCABULARY

(der baanhOf)
der Bahnhof
railroad station

(dee faarkahrten)
die Fahrkarten
ticket/tickets

(daas glays)
das Gleis
track platform

(dee meenoote)
die Minute, die Minuten
minute/minutes

58

DIALOG

Stefan und Ulrike kommen am Bahnhof an. Sie fahren mit dem Zug nach Leipzig.

(do'rt)   *(besooCHen)*
Dort wollen sie Freunde besuchen.
there   *visit*

                                         (tsoog)   *(ahbfart)*
Stefan: Könnten Sie mir bitte sagen, wann der nächste Zug nach Leipzig abfährt.
                                           train   *leave*

Angestellter: Der Zug fährt um 10.19 ab.

Stefan: Wie bitte? Um wie viel Uhr?

Angestellter: Um 10.19

                 (yezt)
Stefan: Wie viel Uhr ist es jetzt?
                 now

Angestellter: Es ist 10.16. Sie haben drei Minuten Zeit.

Stefan sagt zu Ulrike: Es gibt einen Zug in drei Minuten.

Ulrike: Mist! Wir sind zu spät.

          (immer)
Stefan: Es ist immer dasselbe. Wir sind immer zu spät.
         always

Ulrike: Du hast heute morgen schlechte Laune, stimmt's?

Stefan: Das reicht!

Ulrike *(zum Angestellten)*: Um wie viel Uhr fährt der nächste Zug nach Leipzig?

(beko'men)
Diesen Zug bekommen wir nicht mehr.
get

Angestellter: Mal sehen…der nächste Zug nach Leipzig fährt um 13.47 ab.

Ulrike schaut Stefan an.

Stefan: Das ist in Ordnung.

Ulrike *(zum Angestellten)*: In Ordnung, zwei Fahrkarten, bitte.

Angestellter: Einfach oder hin und zurück?

Ulrike: Hin und zurück, bitte. Zweite Klasse.

Angestellter: Das macht 30 Euro.

Hier sind Ihre Fahrkarten.

Ulrike: Danke. Welches Gleis?

(goote rayse)
Angestellter: Gleis acht. Gute Reise!
Have a nice trip!

Stefan *(zu Ulrike)*: Also… möchtest du noch in ein Café gehen?

Ulrike: Mit Vergnügen! Es ist unglaublich. Jetzt hast du gute Laune!

Stefan: Natürlich. Weil wir nicht spät sind. Wir sind früh! Lass uns gehen.

DO YOU UNDERSTAND?

Verstehen Sie das?

Answer True or False to the following statements based on the dialog.

1. Stefan und Ulrike reisen mit dem Flugzeug. _____
   (floogtsoyg)
   plane

2. Stefan fragt, wie viel Uhr es ist. _____
   (fraagt)
   asks

3. Stefan denkt, Ulrike hat schlechte Laune. _____
   (denkt)
   think

4. Ulrike möchte drei Fahrkarten. _____

5. Sie nehmen den Zug hin und zurück. _____

TELLING TIME

Wie viel Uhr ist es?
What time is it?

Expressing time in German is easy. When you want to express the full hour, just say the number and then add the word *Uhr: Es ist vier Uhr.* In colloquial German it is very common to omit the word *Uhr* and to say simply *Es ist eins* or *Es ist zwei.*

In Germany, the 24-hour system of telling time ("military" time as we call it in the U.S.) is usually used on TV and radio, with travel schedules, appointments, and theater and concert times in order to avoid ambiguity. Just subtract 12 to figure out the time you are familiar with in the U.S. (16 hours is 16–12 = 4 PM).

Es ist sieben Uhr morgens.

Es ist zwölf Uhr mittags.

Es ist drei Uhr nachmittags.

Es ist acht Uhr abends.

am Morgen
in the morning

am Mittag
noon

am Nachmittag
in the afternoon

am Abend
in the evening

Here are the ways to add the minutes when you are telling time:

Es ist zwanzig vor
zwölf am Morgen.

Es ist zwanzig nach
sieben am Morgen.

Es ist zehn vor
drei am Nachmittag.

Es ist halb
zehn am Morgen.

When you want to express time beyond the full hour clock simply say the number for the minutes in relation to the full hour with *nach* meaning "past" and *vor* meaning "to".

As in English, the fifteen–minute quarters past and before the full hour are expressed as *Viertel nach* and *Viertel vor*, and the half hour is expressed as *halb*. Notice, however, that in German the half hour is counted towards the next full hour and no other modifier is needed. Expressing time on the 24–hour system is even easier. Just say the full hour with the word *Uhr* and add the number for the minutes.

PRACTICE

Match the times with the clocks. Write the correct letter under each clock.
Wie viel Uhr ist es?

a. Es ist Viertel nach zehn.   b. Es ist Viertel vor Vier.   c. Es ist elf Uhr achtunddreißig.

d. Es ist halb sechs.   e. Es ist acht Uhr siebenundvierzig.

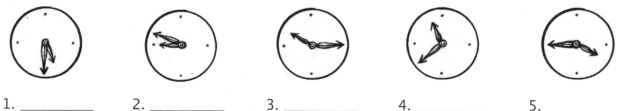

1. _____   2. _____   3. _____   4. _____   5. _____

You'll need to know higher numbers if you want to understand the minutes when someone tells you the time (...not to mention how important these numbers are for shopping or even revealing your age if the situation presents itself.) Read the pronunciation carefully and say each number out loud.

One of the peculiarities of German is that you have to say the second number first before you add the word *und* and then the first digit of the number. So the number 23 is actually expressed as "three-and-twenty", *dreiundzwanzig*.

23	dreiundzwanzig	*(dray-u'nt-zvahntsig)*	40	vierzig	*(feerzig)*
24	vierundzwanzig	*(feer-u'nt-zvahntsig)*	50	fünfzig	*(fünfzig)*
25	fünfundzwanzig	*(fünf-u'nt-zvahntsig)*	60	sechzig	*(seCHzig)*
26	sechsundzwanzig	*(seks-u'nt-zvahntsig)*	70	siebzig	*(seepzig)*
27	siebenundzwanzig	*(seeben-u'nt-zvahntsig)*	71	einundsiebzig	*(ayn-u'nt-seebzig)*
28	achtundzwanzig	*(aCHt-u'nt-zvahntsig)*	72	zweiundsiebzig	*(tsvay-u'nt-seebzig)*
29	neunundzwanzig	*(noyn-u'nt-zvahntsig)*	80	achtzig	*(aCHtzig)*
30	dreißig	*(drayzig)*	90	neunzig	*(noynzig)*
31	einunddreißig	*(ayn-u'nt- drayzig)*	95	fünfundneunzig	*(fünf-u'nt-noynzig)*
32	zweiunddreißig	*(zvay-u'nt- drayzig)*	100	(ein)hundert	*(aynhu'ndert)*

CHAPTER 11

(vahs mahCHst doo in dayner fraytsayt)
Was machst du in deiner Freizeit?
What do you do in your free time?

(blitzblahnk)
blitzblank
neat as a pin

(bay taagesunbru'CH)
bei Tagesanbruch
at the crack of dawn

(ayn riCHtiger gu'rméko'CH)
ein richtiger Gourmetkoch
a real gourmet cook

FOCUS: PREPOSITIONS

in
in

vor
in front of

unter
under

in/drinnen
inside

auf
on

hinter
behind

neben
next to

außen/draußen
outside

USEFUL EXPRESSIONS

(es gipt)
es gibt
there is/there are

(im internet sorfen)
im Internet surfen
surf the Web

(eemal SCHiken)
Email schicken
send email

VOCABULARY

(im Oberen SCHto'kverk)
im oberen Stockwerk
upstairs

(im ertgeSCHo's)
im Erdgeschoss
downstairs

(der hu'nt)
der Hund

(ahlt)
alt
old

(dee loyte)
die Leute
people

(der kompYooter)
der Computer
computer

(Yu'ng, der Yu'nge)
jung, der Junge
young, boy

(dee katse)
die Katze

STORY

Waldi ist ein kleiner, brauner Hund. Er lebt in einem Haus mit einer schwarzen Katze, die

Frida heißt. Drei Leute leben in dem Haus: ein alter Mann, eine Frau, und ein kleiner Junge.

Ihr Haus ist wunderschön und blitzblank. Waldi besucht oft Markus, der sieben Jahre alt

ist, in seinem Kinderzimmer im oberen Stockwerk.

(warend)
Waldi sitzt gern auf dem Bett, während Markus mit
while

(SCHpeelsahCHen)
seinen Spielsachen spielt. Frida, die Katze, schläft
toys

unter dem Bett.

Der Großvater von Markus, der Alfred heißt, ist

gern in der Küche. Er kocht gern.

(herd)
Er ist ein richtiger Gourmetkoch. Waldi sitzt gern neben dem Herd. Er kann dann das gute
stove

(reeCHen)   *(tepiCH)*
Essen riechen. Frida schläft auf dem Teppich vor dem Fenster. Waldi schläft gern lange.
smell   *rug*

Aber die Mutter von Markus, Katrin, stellt schon

bei Tagesanbruch den Computer an. Sie liest ihre

Email oder surft im Internet.

(paapeerko'rp)
Frida schläft im Papierkorb.
wastebasket

(rOmaane)
In ihrer Freizeit arbeitet Katrin gern im Garten und sie liest auch gern Romane.
novels

(klaaveer)   *(ferSCHtekt)*
Markus spielt gern Klavier. Wenn Markus Klavier spielt, versteckt sich Waldi hinter dem
piano   *hide*

Sofa im Wohnzimmer. Frida mag keinen

(larm)
Lärm. Sie geht dann nach draußen und
noise

schläft im Garten. Fast jeden Freitag Abend

gehen Katrin, Alfred und Markus ins obere

Stockwerk. Sie sehen fern, lesen oder

spielen im Familienzimmer Karten.

(vayCHen sesel)
Frida schläft auf einem weichen Sessel und Waldi
soft lounge chair

ruht sich neben der Familie auf dem Boden aus.

Waldi hat ein ziemlich angenehmes Leben.

DO YOU UNDERSTAND?

Verstehen Sie das?

Was macht die Familie gern? (What does the family like to do?) Match the members of the family with the things they like to do. Write the letters in the blanks.

1. Waldi _____

2. Frida _____

3. Katrin _____

4. Alfred _____

5. Markus _____

A. Klavier spielen

B. kochen

C. schlafen

D. auf dem Bett sitzen

E. im Internet surfen

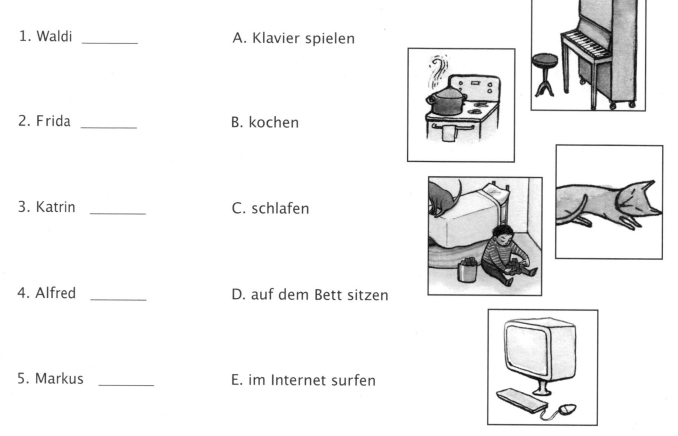

LIEBEN

(leeben)
to love

Note that the German verb *lieben* expresses strong emotional feelings for people. It is not used to describe activities or objects that one might like.

ich liebe	*(iCH leebe)*	*I love*
du liebst	*(doo leepst)*	*you love*
er/sie/es liebt	*(er, zee, es leept)*	*he, she, it loves*
wir lieben	*(veer leeben)*	*we love*
ihr liebt	*(eer leept)*	*you love*
sie lieben	*(zee leeben)*	*they love*
Sie lieben	*(zee leeben)*	*you love (formal)*

PRACTICE

Use the picture to help you fill in the blanks with *in, auf, unter, neben, or hinter.*

1. Der Grossvater ist _____ dem Bett.

2. Es gibt eine Katze _____ dem Bett.

3. Das Bett ist _____ dem Teppich.

4. Das Fenster ist _____ dem Bett.

5. Die Spielsachen sind _____ dem Bett.

6. Es gibt einen Papierkorb _____ dem Bett.

Now write 2 sentences of your own describing the picture.

1. _____.

2. _____.

CHAPTER 12

(vee vahr dayn vo'CHenende)
Wie war dein Wochenende?
Did you have a good weekend?

It's Monday morning. Martin and Monika are at work at the office.

Martin: Guten Morgen, Monika. Hast du ein schönes Wochenende gehabt?

Monika: Hallo, Martin. Ja, es war toll.

Martin: Oh ja? Was hast du gemacht?

Monika: Ich habe am Samstag mit meiner Schwester Tennis gespielt. Am Samstag Abend sind wir ins Konzert gegangen – die Rolling Stones. Es war toll.

Martin: Ich mag ihre Musik. *(érliCH)* Ehrlich gesagt, *to be honest* ich bin überrascht, dass sie immer noch Konzerte geben.

Monika: Ja, sie sind alt, aber immer noch phantastisch. Was hast du am Wochenende gemacht? Hast du wieder Fußball gespielt?

Martin: Ich habe am Samstag Fußball gespielt und gestern habe ich ein bisschen Basketball gespielt. Gestern Abend habe ich mit meinem Neffen einen Film gesehen.

(vahr er goot)
Monika: Oh ja? War er gut?
Was it good?

Martin: Ja. Mein Neffe ist 8 Jahre alt und hatte ein bisschen Angst, aber ich habe den
a little

(u'nterhahltsahm)
Film sehr unterhaltsam gefunden.
entertaining

Monika: Meine Tochter möchte ihn sehen, aber ich sehe lieber romantische Filme.

(virkliCH)
Martin: Wirklich? Ich auch.
really

Monika: Also komm. Du nimmst mich wohl auf den Arm!

Martin: Nein, wirklich! Frage Julia. Sie weiß, dass ich

romantische Filme mag. Tschüss!

Ich muss los. Ich muss mich an die Arbeit machen.

Monika: Julia? Warte! Ich will mehr über dich und Julia wissen!

(gehaymnisen)
Mir reicht's mit euren Geheimnissen.
secrets

(beSCHpreCHu'ng)
Martin: Bis später bei der Besprechung!
meeting

(velCHe)
Monika *(schreit)*: Mist! Welche Besprechung?
which

MATCHING

Match the questions and statements on the left with the appropriate responses on the right.

1. War er gut? _____

2. Ich habe gestern Abend einen Film gesehen. _____

3. Du nimmst mich wohl auf den Arm! _____

4. Hast du ein schönes Wochenende gehabt? _____

5. Wie ist das Konzert gewesen? _____
   How

6. Was hast du am Wochenende gemacht? _____

a) Ja, es war toll.

b) Ich habe Fußball gespielt.

c) Es war phantastisch!

d) Nein, wirklich!

e) Welchen Film hast du gesehen?

f) Ja.

FOCUS: PAST TENSE

There are several past tenses in German, as there are in English. The *Perfekt* is most commonly used as the past tense in spoken German. It is a compound tense, which means it is made up of two parts: a helping verb, *haben* (to have) or *sein* (to be), and a past participle such as *gespielt* (played) or *gegangen* (gone).

To form the *Perfekt,* use the present tense of the helping verb plus a past participle. All regular verbs form their past participles by adding a ge-prefix at the beginning of the verb and a t-suffix at the end of the verb stem. Irregular verbs add a ge-prefix at the beginning of the verb and an en-suffix at the end of the verb. In addition, almost all irregular verbs undergo a vowel change. Can you know if a verb is irregular? No, you cannot. Irregular verbs have to be memorized. However, most of the verbs that are irregular in English are irregular in German as well.

Verb: spielen *(regular)*   Perfekt: Ich habe ge-spiel-t.
Verb: sagen *(regular)*   Perfekt: Ich habe ge-sag-t.
Verb: gehen *(irregular)*   Perfekt: Ich bin ge-gang-en.
Verb: nehmen *(irregular)*   Perfekt: Ich habe ge-nomm-en.

(SCHpeelen)
SPIELEN
to play

ich habe gespielt	*(iCH haabe geSCHpeelt)*	*I played*
du hast gespielt	*(doo hahst geSCHpeelt)*	*you played*
er, sie, es hat gespielt	*(er, zee, es haht geSCHpeelt)*	*he, she, one played*
wir haben gespielt	*(veer haaben geSCHpeelt)*	*we played*
ihr habt gespielt	*(eer hahpt geSCHpeelt)*	*you played*
sie haben gespielt	*(zee haaben geSCHpeelt)*	*they played*
Sie haben gespielt	*(zee haaben geSCHpeelt)*	*you played (formal)*

You might have noticed that the parts of the compound form are spread out through the sentence. The helping verb remains in the position of the conjugated verb while the participle is moved to the end of the sentence.

Moreover, when the *Perfekt* is formed on verbs with separable prefixes such as *anrufen* (to call, to telephone) or *fernsehen* (to watch TV), the ge- is inserted between the prefix and the verb. Carefully study the differences in the following sentences in terms of word order and compound form.

Present Tense: Ich sehe den Film.

Perfekt: Ich habe den Film gesehen.

Present Tense: Er sieht im Wohnzimmer fern.

Perfekt: Er hat im Wohnzimmer ferngesehen.

(géhen)
GEHEN
to go

Perfekt of gehen

ich bin gegangen	*(iCH bin gegahngen)*	*I went*
du bist gegangen	*(doo bist gegahngen)*	*you went*
er/sie/es ist gegangen	*(er, zee, es ist gegahngen)*	*he/she/one went*
wir sind gegangen	*(veer sint gegahngen)*	*we went*
ihr seid gegangen	*(eer sayt gegahngen)*	*you went*
sie sind gegangen	*(zee sint gegahngen)*	*they went*
Sie sind gegangen	*(zee sint gegahngen)*	*you went (formal)*

PRACTICE

Read the following paragraph. Some of the verbs are missing. Look at the pictures and write what each person did in the blanks. Use the Perfekt for all the verbs. That is, take the present tense of **haben** (have) or **sein** (be). (Look at the verb boxes on the previous page for help.) Then choose the past participle from the list.

Examples: Gestern _____ ich eine Pizza _____ . (ate)
            Yesterday

Gestern habe ich eine Pizza gegessen.

Er _____ ins Kino _____ . (went)

Er ist ins Kino gegangen.

Choose one of these words to complete your past tense verbs.

geschwommen (haben)   gegangen (sein)   gemacht (haben)
angerufen (haben)   ferngesehen (haben)   gespielt (haben)   gesprochen (haben)

Gestern _____ ich meine Freundin _____ .

Wir _____ lange über das Wochenende _____ (talked/spoke).

Sie ist sehr müde gewesen.

Sie _____ den ganzen Morgen

Fußball _____ (played).

Am Sonntag ist sie zu Hause geblieben und

_____ _____ (watched TV).

Dann hat sie mich gefragt: "Was _____ du _____?"

Ich habe ihr gesagt:

"Mein Freund und ich _____ in einem See _____ (swam).

Und am Samstag Abend _____ wir auf

eine Party _____." (went)

CHAPTER 13

(vahs moCHtest doo essen)
Was möchtest du essen?
What do you want to eat?

(barenhu'nger)
Ich habe einen Bärenhunger.
I could eat a horse.

(prost) (zu'm vOl)
Prost! Zum Wohl!
Cheers!

(ahpeteet)
Guten Appetit!
Have a good meal!

VOCABULARY

(milCH)
die Milch
milk

(beer)
das Bier
beer

(kahfé)
der Kaffee
a coffee

(tay)
der Tee
tea

(vayn)
der Wein
wine

(Opst)
das Obst
fruit

(ahpfel)
die Äpfel
apple

(bahnaanen)
die Bananen
banana

(ahnahnahs)
die Ananas
pineapple

(érdbeeren)
die Erdbeeren
strawberry

(kirSCHen)
die Kirschen
cherry

(zveebeln)
die Zwiebeln
onion

(naaCHtiSCH)
der Nachtisch
dessert

(ays)
das Eis
ice cream

(fiSCH)
der Fisch
fish

(kooCHen)
der Kuchen
cake

(brOt)
das Brot
bread

(rays)
der Reis
rice

(po'm frits)
die Pommes Frites
french fries

(flaySCH)
das Fleisch
meat

(hoon)
das Huhn
poultry

(rindflaySCH)
das Rindfleisch
beef

(SCHinken)
der Schinken
ham

(kaze)
der Käse
cheese

(kuro'ten)
die Karotten
carrot

(piltse)
die Pilze
mushroom

(to'maaten)
die Tomaten
tomato

(gemüze)
das Gemüse
vegetables

(zu'pe)
die Suppe
soup

(zahlaat)
der Salat
salad

STORY

Drei Freunde sind in einem Restaurant: Horst, Uwe und Karsten.

Horst: Was möchtet ihr essen?

Uwe: Ich habe keinen großen Hunger. Vielleicht eine Suppe und einen Salat.

Horst: Und du, Karsten?

Karsten: Ich? Ich habe einen Bärenhunger! Ich habe heute Morgen nicht gefrühstückt.

Horst: Wirklich? Warum nicht?
really

(oufgevahCHt)
Karsten: Ich bin spät aufgewacht und hatte keine Zeit zum Essen.
wake up

Ich bin sogar zu spät zur Arbeit gekommen.

Kellner: Möchten Sie jetzt bestellen?　　　　**Uwe:** Was für Suppe haben Sie heute?
order　　　　　　　　　　　　　　　　　*what kind of*

Kellner: Unsere Tagessuppe ist Pilzsuppe.　　**Uwe:** Das hört sich gut an. Ich möchte
　　　　　　　　　　　　　　　　　　　　　　Suppe und einen grünen Salat.

Kellner: Ist das alles?　　　　　　　　　　**Uwe:** Ja, danke.

　　　　　　　　　　　　　　　　　(kaze-o'mlet)
Kellner: Und für Sie?　　**Horst:** Ich hätte gern ein Käseomelette und einen Tomatensalat.

Kellner: Sonst noch etwas? **Horst:** Ja, zum Nachtisch hätte ich gern ein Stück Apfelkuchen.
   anything else

Kellner: Und für Sie?

(SCHvahrzvalder)
Karsten: Als Vorspeise hätte ich gern den Schwarzwälder Schinken mit Brot. Dann hätte ich
   black forest

gern das Huhn in Weißweinsoße. Und zum Nachtisch möchte ich Kirschpudding.

(fo'relle)
Kellner: Es tut mir leid, aber Huhn haben wir nicht mehr. Wie wäre es mit Forelle?
   trout

Karsten: In Ordnung, ich nehme die Forelle.

Kellner: Hätten Sie gern eine Nachspeise bestellt?

Karsten: Ja, ich hätte gern das Vanilleeis.

Horst: Wir hätten auch gern eine Flasche Weißwein.

Kellner: Gern.

Horst, Uwe und Karsten: Zum Wohl!

Horst, Uwe und Karsten: Guten Appetit!

PRACTICE

FOOD VOCABULARY

Use the clues in English to find the words in German.

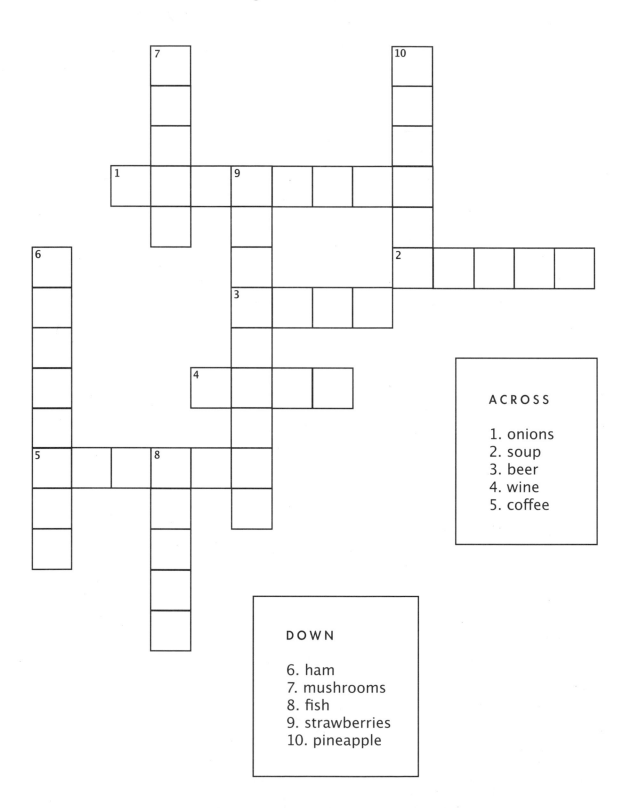

ACROSS

1. onions
2. soup
3. beer
4. wine
5. coffee

DOWN

6. ham
7. mushrooms
8. fish
9. strawberries
10. pineapple

REVIEW

Richtig oder falsch?
true or false

1. Uwe hat großen Hunger. _____

2. Apfelkuchen ist ein Nachtisch. _____

3. Horst bestellt Rotwein. _____

4. Uwe isst Huhn. _____

5. Uwe möchte Erdbeertorte zum Nachtisch. _____

FOCUS

The following words and expressions might be
helpful when ordering or buying food in Germany:

ein Glas Milch	*a glass of milk*
eine Flasche Bier	*a bottle of beer*
eine Dose Cola	*a can of coke*
ein Becher Joghurt	*a container of yogurt*
ein Stück Kuchen	*a piece of cake*
eine Scheibe Brot	*a slice of bread*
ein Teller Suppe	*a cup/bowl of soup*

CHAPTER 14

(vahs ist lOs)
Was ist los?
What's the matter?

> **Ich bin erschöpft.**
> *I'm exhausted.*

> **Herzlichen Glückwunsch zum Geburtstag!**
> *Happy Birthday!*

> (vahs ist lOs)
> **Was ist los?**
> *What's the matter?*

> (füle)
> **Ich fühle mich nicht gut.**
> *I don't feel well.*

VOCABULARY

(fayern)	(erkaltu'ng)	(krahnk)	(gezu'nthayt)	(tsoonéhmen)
feiern	die Erkältung	krank	die Gesundheit	zunehmen
celebrate	*a cold*	*sick*	*health*	*to gain weight*

DIALOG

Drei Freunde treffen sich in dem Haus von Bettina, um Christines Geburtstag zu feiern.

Bettina: Hallo, Christine. Herzlichen Glückwunsch zum Geburtstag!

Christine: Hallo, Bettina. Danke! Heute ist so ein schöner Tag.

Essen wir draußen zu Mittag?

Bettina: Ja, im Garten.

Gabi: Hallo!

Bettina: Gabi, was ist los?!
what's the matter

Gabi: Ich fühle mich nicht gut.

Bettina: Hast du eine Erkältung?

Gabi: *(vaarSCHaynliCH)*
Ja, wahrscheinlich.
probably

Mein Hals tut weh und

ich bin völlig erledigt.

Ich weiß nicht, ob ich zu Arbeit gehen kann.

(gloube)
Ich glaube, ich bleibe heute Nachmittag zu Hause.
think

Bettina: Wie lange bist du schon krank?   **Gabi:** Seit zwei Tagen.
How long   *for*

Bettina: *(vahru'm)*
Warum bist du denn gekommen?
why   come

Gabi: Heute ist doch Christines Geburtstag!

Ich möchte mit euch zusammen feiern!
together

Christine: Oh Gabi, das ist wirklich lieb von dir! Vielen Dank.

Gabi: Wie geht es dir, Christine? Du warst doch letzten Monat krank.

Christine: Es geht mir gut. Ich habe *(sOgaar)* sogar etwas *(tsoogenomen)* zugenommen. Ich fahre jetzt auch
even
jeden Tag mit dem Fahrrad zur Arbeit.

Gabi: Das ist phantastisch. Du siehst wirklich *(grOsahrtig)* großartig aus.
great
Und was macht deine Arbeit?

Christine: Ich habe zu viel zu tun, aber meine Arbeit ist sehr interessant.

Ich treffe jeden Tag neue Leute.

Gabi: Das ist schön!

Bettina: Das Mittagessen ist fertig!

Wir haben Kartoffelsalat, Wiener Würstchen, Brot, Käse, und zum

Nachtisch werden wir Schokoladentorte haben. Lasst uns mit einem Glas

(ahnfahngen)
Champagner anfangen.
begin

Gabi, Christine, Bettina: Zum Wohl!

Gabi, Bettina: Auf Christines vierzigsten Geburtstag!

Christine: Und auf Gabis Gesundheit!

(SCHOn)
Gabi: Ich fühle mich schon viel besser!
already

JA ODER NEIN?

Read in English. Answer in German.

_____ 1. Does Gabi have a sore throat?

_____ 2. Does Christine like her job?

_____ 3. Is the celebration at Gabi's house?

_____ 4. Is it Christine's thirtieth birthday?

_____ 5. Was Christine sick last month?

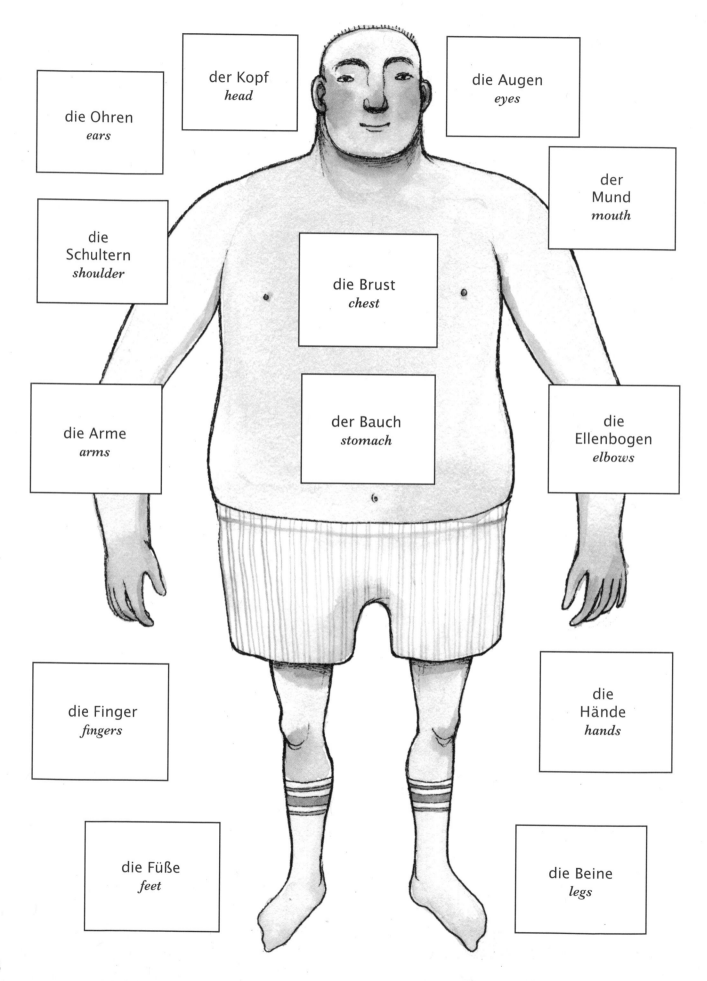

die Ohren
ears

der Kopf
head

die Augen
eyes

der Mund
mouth

die Schultern
shoulder

die Brust
chest

die Arme
arms

der Bauch
stomach

die Ellenbogen
elbows

die Finger
fingers

die Hände
hands

die Füße
feet

die Beine
legs

86

PRACTICE

As in English, there are two ways to express physical pain in German. You can either say the body part and then add the verbal phrase *weh tun* (to hurt) to it as in *Mein Hals tut weh*; Or you add the word *Schmerzen* (ache) to the noun describing the body part that is hurting as in *Ich habe Zahnschmerzen*. Note that the noun *Schmerzen* is usually used without an article in German.

Remember that Gabi said, *"Mein Hals tut weh."* See if you can match the English with the German by looking at the diagram. Write the letters in the blanks.

1. Ich habe Bauchschmerzen.   _____
2. Mein Knie tut weh.   _____
3. Ich habe Kopfschmerzen.   _____
4. Meine Füße tun weh.   _____
5. Ich habe Zahnschmerzen.   _____
6. Meine Augen tun weh.   _____
7. Mein Hals tut weh.   _____
8. Ich habe Rückenschmerzen.   _____

a. My feet hurt.
b. My eyes hurt.
c. I have a stomachache.
d. My back hurts.
e. My neck hurts.
f. My knee hurts.
g. I have a headache.
h. I have a toothache.

FOCUS

In the expression *Ich fühle mich krank* the reflexive pronoun mich is added to the verb *fühlen* and refers back to the speaking subject. English examples of reflexive verbs are "to enjoy oneself" or "to behave oneself". Most of the time, the use of a reflexive pronoun depends on whether the verb refers back to the subject of the sentence or to an object. Compare "I cut myself" with "I cut the potatoes". There are cases, however, when the reflexive pronoun is part of the verb, and omitting the reflexive pronoun would either change the meaning of the verb or produce an incorrect phrase as in "to pride oneself" or "to busy oneself". There are many more of these standardized reflexive verbs in German than there are in English. As in English (myself, yourself, himself etc.), the subject and the reflexive pronoun have to agree:

Ich fühle mich krank.   Wir fühlen uns krank.
Du fühlst dich krank.   Ihr fühlt euch krank.
Er/sie/es fühlt sich krank.   Sie fühlen sich krank.

FÜHLEN *to feel*		
ich fühle	(iCH fühle)	*I feel*
du fühlst	(doo fühlst)	*you feel*
er, sie, es fühlt	(er, zee, es fühlt)	*he, she, one feels*
wir fühlen	(veer fühlen)	*we feel*
ihr fühlt	(eehr fühlt)	*you feel*
sie fühlen	(zee fühlen)	*they feel*
Sie fühlen	(zee fühlen)	*you feel (formal)*

(dahs Schtet dir ousgezaySCHnet)
Das steht dir ausgezeichnet!
That looks great on you!

(fraage)
Das kommt (gar) nicht in Frage!
No way!

(ahngebOt)
Im Angebot
On sale

VOCABULARY

(baade-ahnzook)
der Badeanzug
swimsuit

(teeSCHort)
das T–Shirt

(dSCHeens)
die Jeans

(tu'rnSCHoo-e)
die Turnschuhe
tennis shoes

(pu'lo've'r)
der Pullover
sweater

(SCHtru'mpfhOse)
die Strumpfhose
pantyhose

(fleege)
die Fliege
bowtie

(klayt)
das Kleid
dress

(SCHteefel)
die Stiefel
boots

(büstenhahlter)
der Büstenhalter
bra

(u'nterhOse)
die Unterhose
underpants, slip

(SCHlaafahnzook)
der Schlafanzug
pajama

(baademahntel)
der Bademantel
bathrobe

(housSCHoo-e)
die Hausschuhe
slippers

(hahnttahSCHe)
die Handtasche
purse

(ku'rze hOse)
die kurze Hose
shorts

(SCHaal)
der Schal
scarf

(hoot)
der Hut
hat

(hemt)
das Hemd
shirt

(mahntel)
der Mantel
coat

(krahvahte)
die Krawatte
tie

(blooze)
die Bluse
blouse

(blazer)
der Blazer
blazer

(hahntSCHoo-e)
die Handschuhe
gloves

(regenSCHirm)
der
Regenschirm
umbrella

(ro'k)
der Rock
skirt

(hOze)
die Hose
pants

(SCHteefel)
die Stiefel
boots

(SCHoo-e)
die Schuhe
shoes

DIALOG

Norbert und Ursula Meier machen im nächsten Monat in Italien Ferien. Sie kaufen neue Kleidung ein. Sie sind gerade in einem Geschäft für Herrenbekleidung. Norbert probiert einen grauen Anzug an.

(pahst)
Ursula: Der Anzug passt dir gut, aber willst du wirklich einen Anzug mitbringen?
fit

(féree-en) *(fo'rmel)*
Norbert: Du hast wahrscheinlich Recht. Für die Ferien ist ein Anzug zu formell.
vacation

(zee)
Ursula: Zieh diese weiße Hose und das rosa Hemd an.

Norbert: Rosa? Das kommt gar nicht in Frage! Gib mir bitte ein blaues Hemd.

(helfen)
Verkäufer: Kann ich Ihnen helfen?   **Norbert:** Haben Sie dieses Hemd in Blau?
help

(deeselbe)
Verkäufer: Dieselbe Größe?   **Norbert:** Ja.
the same

Verkäufer: Hier, bitte.

Norbert: Das sieht viel besser aus.

Ich brauche auch einen Blazer.

(geraade)
Verkäufer: Dieser hier ist gerade im Angebot.
now

Ursula: Der ist chic. Oh, der steht

dir wirklich gut!

Norbert: Also gut, ich hätte gern das Hemd,

die Hose und den Blazer.

(tsaalen) *(kahse)*
Verkäufer: Bitte zahlen Sie dort an der Kasse.
pay *cash register*

(geSCHaft)
Norbert und Ursula sind jetzt in einem Geschäft für Damenbekleidung.
store

(prObeert)
Ursula probiert ein gelbes Kleid an.
try

(hüpSCH)
Norbert: Das Kleid ist wirklich hübsch, aber es ist zu lang.
pretty

(feelayCHt)
Ursula: Vielleicht… Entschuldigung, haben Sie dieses Kleid in
maybe

einer kleineren Größe?

(toot mir layd)
Verkäuferin: Nein, tut mir Leid, wir haben es nur in dieser Größe.
I am sorry

Norbert: Hier ist ein rotes Kleid.

(fu'rCHtbaar)   *(traage)*
Ursula: Das Kleid ist furchtbar! So etwas trage ich nicht!
ugly   *wear*

Norbert: Mir gefällt es auch nicht.

Verkäuferin: Gefällt Ihnen dieser Rock? Das ist der letzte und er ist in Ihrer Größe.

Ursula: Der Rock gefällt mir sehr gut.

Norbert: Probier ihn an!

Verkäuferin: Hier ist eine gelbe Bluse und ein Seidenschal.
(saydenSCHaal)
silk scarf

Ursula: Hm ... was meinst du?
(maynst)
think

Norbert: Das steht dir ausgezeichnet!

Ursula: Gut. Sehen wir uns noch Badeanzüge an. Dann kann der Urlaub anfangen.
(oorloub)
vacation

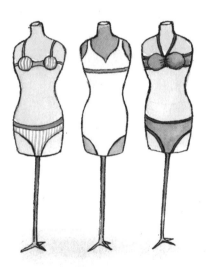

DO YOU UNDERSTAND?

Which of these statements describe the situations in the dialogs?
Put a check next to the sentences that are true.

1. _____ Norbert kauft ein rosa Hemd.   2. _____ Ursula gefällt das Hemd.

3. _____ Norbert probiert einen Regenmantel an.   4. _____ Norbert und Ursula fahren nach Italien.

5. _____ Norbert sagt, das gelbe Kleid ist zu klein.

PRACTICE

Each of the 5 words below is a scrambled word for a piece of women's clothing. Unscramble each of the clue words. Copy the letters in the numbered cells to other cells with the same number. Then you will find the answer to the question! (The answer does not refer to the dialogs in this chapter. This is just to practice some of the new words you learned.)

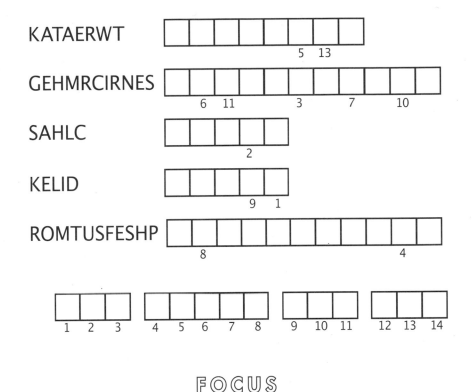

FOCUS

The demonstrative pronouns are used to identify an object among a group of things or to put special emphasis on a particular object. The endings of demonstrative pronouns have to agree with the number, gender and case of the nouns they are preceding. The following examples list the demonstrative pronouns in the nominative case for the nouns *der Mantel* (masculine), *die Bluse* (feminine), and *das Kleid* (neuter).

Singular:	dieser Mantel, diese Bluse, dieses Kleid	*this coat, this blouse, this dress*
Plural:	diese Mäntel/Blusen/Kleider	*these coats, these blouses, these dresses*
Singular:	jener Mantel, jene Bluse, jenes Kleid	*that coat, that blouse, that dress*
Plural:	jene Mäntel/Blusen/Kleider	*those coats, those blouses, those dresses*

In colloquial German, it is very common to use the definite article instead of the demonstrative pronouns. Especially the forms *jener/eles* are generally avoided.

Wie gefällt dir dieser Mantel?	*How do you like this coat?*
Der hier gefällt mir besser.	*This one here I like better.*
Und wie gefällt dir dieses Kleid?	*And how do you like this dress?*
Das gefällt mir gar nicht.	*I don't like this one at all.*

CHAPTER 16

(zO ist dahs leben hahlt)
So ist das Leben halt!
That's Life!

No matter how much you prepare for a trip *(Reise)* to a foreign country, there will often be some unexpected things that can happen. When some of these things are unfortunate or unpleasant, it helps to know some of the language *(Sprache)* in order to understand *(verstehen)* what people like doctors *(Ärzte)* or police *(Polizei)* are asking. You might also need to explain *(erklären)* what happened. A good attitude goes a long way in preparing you to cope with unfortunate circumstances. Accepting an unforeseen event as part of your experience will help you get through it. You will see in the story in this chapter how Robert from New York handles his problems *(Probleme)* on a business trip to Berlin.

(SCHrekliCH)
Wie schrecklich!
What a terrible thing!

(leeber SCHpat ahls gaar niCHt)
Lieber spät als gar nicht!
Better late than never!

VOCABULARY

(ko'mpYooter)
der Computer
computer

(dru'ker)
der Drucker
printer

(fahks)
das Fax
fax

(handi)
das Handy
cell phone

(tahs-tah-toor)
das Tastatur
keyboard

(mous)
die Maus
mouse

STORY

(rayse) *(pahseert)*
Lies, was Robert auf seiner Reise nach Berlin passiert ist.
trip *happened*

(glük) *(geSCHaftsrayse)*
Mein Bruder Robert hat kein Glück. Im letzten Monat hat er eine Geschäftsreise nach Berlin
luck *business trip*

gemacht.

(flooghaafen)
Zuerst hat man seinen Laptop am Flughafen gestohlen. Wie schrecklich!
airport

(SCHef)
Dann wollte er ein Fax an sein Büro in New York schicken, aber sein Chef hat es nicht
boss

(fersooCHt) *(naariCHt)* *(unroofbeuntwo'rter)*
bekommen. Er hat versucht, eine Nachricht auf dem Anrufbeantworter in seinem
try *message* *answering machine*

(klahpte) *(ahls)*
Büro zu hinterlassen, aber das klappte auch nicht. Als er in Berlin angekommen war,
worked *when*

(ferirt)
hat er sich sehr geärgert. Er hat sich nämlich verirrt und ist 40 Minuten zu spät zu
got lost

(beSChpreCHu'ng)
seiner ersten Besprechung gekommen.
meeting

Als jemand gesagt hat "Lieber spät als gar nicht", hat er das zuerst nicht verstanden.

(SCHleesliCH)
Als er es schließlich verstanden hat, fühlte er sich ein bisschen besser.
finally

(zoomindest)   *(erfo'lg)*   *(aynige)*
Zumindest hatte er Erfolg mit seinen Emails an seinen Chef, seine Familie und einige
at least   *success*   *some*

Freunde. Er hat ein Internet-Cafe nahe bei seinem Hotel gefunden. Dort konnte er fast

jeden Abend die Computer benutzen. Mein Bruder hat gesagt, dass dort immer sehr viele

Leute waren, die Emails schickten oder im Internet surften.

                                              (tahs-tah-toor) *(ahnders)*
Robert konnte aber nicht sehr schnell schreiben, denn die Tastatur war anders.
                                                  keyboard   *different*

(bezitser)
Dem Besitzer hat das nicht besonders gefallen.
    owner

                                  (gemeetet)
Am Samstag hat Robert ein Auto gemietet, um auf das Land zu fahren und ein Picknick
                                  rent

an einem Fluss zu machen. Leider hatte sein Auto auf der Autobahn eine Panne. *(pahne)*
breakdown

Am Sonntag hat er ein Fahrrad gemietet und ist zu einem großen Park gefahren.

Es hat fast die ganze Zeit geregnet und auf dem Rückweg hat sein Fahrrad einen Platten *(fahst)* *(rükweg)* *(plahtten)*
almost *way back* *flat tire*

bekommen. Armer Robert. Aber selbst wenn er Pech hat, sagt mein Bruder immer: *(aarmer)*
poor *even* *bad luck*

"So ist das Leben halt."

DO YOU UNDERSTAND?

Match the phrases on the left with the words on the right.

1. "Lieber spät als gar nicht." _____   a) Maus und Tastatur

2. hat sein Chef nicht bekommen _____   b) Internet-Café

3. hatte auf der Autobahn eine Panne _____   c) die Besprechung

4. hatte einen Platten _____   d) Laptop Computer

5. von hier schickte er Emails _____   e) das Auto

6. hat man gestohlen _____   f) das Fahrrad

g) das Fax

MATCHING

See if you can match the past tense verb with the meaning. Look back at the story for help. Use the same form as in the story. Just use the past participle (not the helping words).

_____   1. gefunden   a) rented

_____   2. gemietet   b) stolen

_____   3. verirrt   c) tried

_____   4. verstanden   d) found

_____   5. bekommen   e) lost

_____   6. angekommen   f) understood

_____   7. gestohlen   g) arrived

_____   8. versucht   h) received

FOCUS

(nOtful)
der Notfall
emergency

Was ist passiert?
What happened?

(hilfe)
Hilfe!
Help!

Man hat (mein Auto) gestohlen.
They stole (my car).

(deep)
Dieb!
Thief!

Ich möchte einen Unfall melden …
I want to report an accident…

(po'litsay)
Polizei!
Police!

Rufen Sie die Feuerwehr an!
Call the fire department!

(foyer)
Feuer!
Fire!

Ich habe (meine Brieftasche) verloren.
I've lost my (wallet).

FOCUS

Find 4 emergency words in the puzzle. Then circle them.

r	v	f	d	a	x	a	w	u	g
g	w	o	e	h	f	e	k	n	o
i	p	o	l	i	z	e	i	o	w
v	f	x	s	l	u	q	l	t	r
s	u	s	j	f	u	q	i	f	t
q	i	z	x	e	w	r	g	a	i
d	p	o	l	i	c	e	u	l	g
g	f	e	u	e	r	p	r	l	g

Be sure to use the accompanying "phrase" stickers to practice what you've learned. Place them around your work and home. Build on the foundation this book provides by immersing yourself in German as much as you can. German radio and television programs may be available in your area. German films are another enjoyable way to hear the language. Read anything you can find in German, including children's books, easy novels, comics, magazines, newspapers, and even the labels on household products. Search the Internet for German websites that will give you countless opportunities to read and listen to German.

ANSWER KEY

CHAPTER 1:

Practice:
Klaus geht zum Abendessen.
Wo möchtest du frühstücken.
Zum Mittagessen möchte Sabine ein Brötchen essen.
Wo möchtest du essen?

Matching: 1. c   2. f   3. c   4. b   5. e   6. d

CHAPTER 2:

Practice:
4 (vier) – 10 (zehn) – 5 (fünf) – 3 (drei) – 1 (eins) – 7 (sieben) – 8 (acht) – 9 (neun)

Practice:
Anna und ihre Freundin essen in einem Restaurant.
Juliane hat zwei Brötchen.
Peter betritt das Restaurant.
Peter ist sehr glücklich.

CHAPTER 3:

Practice:
Wie alt bist du?   Ich bin zehn Jahre alt.
Woher kommen Sie?   Ich komme aus Seattle.
Wie heißt du?   Ich heiße Anke.
Wie heißen Sie?   Ich heiße Sylvia Bauer.

Practice:
Wie heißt du?
Du hast Hunger?
Hast du Hunger?
Woher kommst du?
Isst du Pizza?
Wie alt bist du?

CHAPTER 4:

Verstehen Sie das?
Brigitte is German.
The clerk speaks to fast.
John wants to buy two rolls.
Brigitte is asking for mineral water.
The scene takes place in a bakery.

Was möchten Sie?
elf – achtzehn – fünfzehn – drei – fünf – zwei

CHAPTER 5:

Practice:
Jan und Monika wohnen in einem großen blauen und rosa Haus.
Jan ist 25 Jahre alt.
Im Allgemeinen ist Jan sehr nett.
Monika ist Geschäftsfrau.
Jan gefällt seine Arbeit nicht.
Monika fährt mit dem Zug nach Stuttgart.
Jan fährt mit dem Auto nach Freiburg.

Practice: Crossword Puzzle

Across	Down
1. gelb	2. grün
2. grau	5. rot
3. braun	6. rosa
4. orange	7. weiß
	8. blau

Practice:

_3_ Mittwoch   _7_ Sonntag   _2_ Dienstag   _5_ Freitag

    _1_ Montag   _6_ Samstag   _4_ Donnerstag

CHAPTER 6:

Wer hat das Rennen gewonnen?
A – der Erste
B – der Zweite
C – der Dritte
D – der Vierte
E – der Fünfte
F – der Sechste
G – der Siebte
H – der Achte
I – Neunte
J – Zehnte

CHAPTER 7:

Practice:
Mein Vater macht liebe im Winter Ferien.
Mein Bruder Uwe, der 17 Jahre alt ist, wandert gern im Wald.
Wann machen wir Ferien?
Manchmal gehen wir auch im Winter und im Frühling wandern.
Ich bin 20 Jahre alt.
Es mag die Farben des Herbstes (orange, rot, gelb und braun).
Ich auch! Ich und Marion mögen all die schönen Blumen.
Im Juni, Juli und August gehen wir oft an den Strand.

Practice:

die Schwester	der Mann
der Strand	der Morgen
die Familie	die Jahreszeit
der Käse	das Museum
das Auto	die Straße

CHAPTER 8:

Practice:
Peter

1.
a) Bernd
b) der Bruder

2.
a) Kerstin
b) die Schwägerin

3.
a) Siegfried
b) der Vater

4.
a) Gerda
b) die Mutter

5.
a) Andrea
b) die Ehefrau

6.
a) Elisabeth
b) die Schwiegermutter

7.
a) Albert
b) der Schwiegervater

8.
a) Nicole
b) die Tochter

Focus: 1) Andrea 2) Gerda 3) Bernd 4) Nicole 5) Peter

Adjectives:
die große Frau
die kleinen Männer
die gut aussehenden Töchter
der kleine Hut
die blauen Hüte
der intelligente Vater

Possessive Adjectives:
1. meine Familie
2. sein Haus
3. ihr Vater
4. deine Schwester
5. ihre Brüder
6. Ihr Hut
7. meine Freunde
8. ihre Mutter
9. seine Frau
10. unsere Eltern

CHAPTER 9:

Verstehen Sie das?
Wem ist kalt? – Es ist Liesel kalt.
Wo ist Liesel? – Liesel ist in Alaska.
Wo regnet es? – Es regnet in Fulda.
Wann arbeitet Liesel? – Liesel arbeitet jeden Tag außer am Sonntag.
Wann möchte ihre Mutter nach Alaska kommen? – Sie möchte im Sommer kommen.

Practice:
Mother: 1, 6, 7
Daughter: 2, 3, 4, 5, 8

Practice:
Es ist heiß im Sommer.
Es regnet viel im April.
Es ist furchtbares Wetter im November.
Es schneit im Januar.
Es ist windig im Frühling.
Heute ist es schön.

Practice and Review:
Schnee
kalt
viel
hier
Frühling

CHAPTER 10:

Verstehen Sie das?
F (Sie reisen mit dem Zug.)
T
F (Stefan hat schlechte Laune.)
F (Ulrike möchte zwei Fahrkarten.)
T

Practice:
1. d
2. e
3. a
4. c
5. b

CHAPTER 11:

Verstehen Sie das?
1 D
2 C
3 E
4 B
5 A

Practice:
1. in 2. auf 3. auf 4. hinter 5. unter 6. neben

CHAPTER 12:

Matching:
1. f
2. e
3. d
4. a
5. c
6. b

Practice:

Gestern <u>habe</u> ich meine Freundin <u>angerufen</u>. Wir <u>haben</u> lange über das Wochenende <u>gesprochen</u>. Sie ist sehr müde gewesen. Sie <u>hat</u> den ganzen Morgen Fußball <u>gespielt</u>. Am Sonntag ist sie zu Hause geblieben und <u>hat</u> <u>ferngesehen</u>. Dann hat sie mich gefragt: "Was <u>hast</u> du <u>gemacht</u>?" Ich habe ihr gesagt: "Mein Freund und ich <u>sind</u> in einem See <u>geschwommen</u>. Und am Samstag Abend <u>sind</u> wir auf eine Party <u>gegangen</u>."

CHAPTER 13:

Crossword:

Across:	Down:
1. zwiebeln	6. schinken
2. suppe	7. pilze
3. bier	8. fisch
4. wein	9. erdbeeren
5. kaffee	10. ananas

Review:
T
T
F (Horst bestellt Weißwein.)
F (Uwe isst Forelle.)
F (Uwe isst keinen Nachtisch.)

CHAPTER 14:

Ja oder Nein?
1. Ja, Gabis Hals tut weh.
2. Ja, Christines Arbeit ist sehr interessant.
3. Nein, der Geburtstag ist in Bettinas Haus.
4. Nein, es ist Christines vierzigster Geburtstag.
5. Ja, Christine war letzten Monat krank.

Practice:
1. c
2. f
3. g
4. a
5. h
6. b
7. e
8. d

CHAPTER 15:

Do you understand?
1. F (Das rosa Hemd gefällt Norbert nicht.)
2. T
3. F (Norbert probiert keinen Regenmantel an.)
4. T
5. F (Das Kleid ist zu klein.)

Puzzle:
Krawatte (tie)
Regenschirm (umbrella)
Schal (scarf)
Kleid (dress)
Strumpfhose (pantyhose)
The answer is: Das steht dir gut. (That looks great on you.)

CHAPTER 16:

Do you understand?
1. c
2. g
3. e
4. a
5. f
6. b
7. d

Matching:
1. d
2. a
3. e
4. f
5. h
6. g
7. b
8. c

GLOSSARY

CHAPTER 1:

das Abendessen – dinner
das Auto – car
das Bett – bed
das Brötchen – breakfast roll
essen – to eat
das Fleisch – meat
die Frau – woman
das Frühstück – breakfast
frühstücken – to have breakfast
können – can
der Mann – man
miteinander – together
das Mittagessen – lunch
möchten – to like to
der Morgen – morning
nehmen – to take
die Pasta – pasta
sprechen – to say, to speak
der Strand – beach
wo – where
wollen – to want
zu – to, for
der Zug – train

Expressions:
Es macht mir nichts aus. – I don't care.
Es ist mir egal. – It doesn't matter to me.
Lass uns gehen. – Let's go.
Guten Morgen. – Guten Morgen.
Wie geht es dir? – How are you?
Es geht mir gut. – I am fine.

CHAPTER 2:

die Freundinnen – (female) friends
der Käse – cheese
betreten – to enter
verlassen – to leave
geben – to give
glücklich – happy
traurig – sad
das Restaurant – restaurant
vorstellen – to introduce
freuen – to be pleased
kennenlernen – to get to know
sagen – to say
fragen – to ask
erwidern – to respond

Expressions:
Ich habe Hunger. – I am hungry.

Was für ein Glück! – What luck!

CHAPTER 3:

alt – old
aus – out off, from
ein wenig – a little
heißen – to be named
hier – here
ja – yes
das Jahr – year
kommen – to come
nein – no
der Sohn – son
sprechen – to speak, to say
die Tochter – daughter
und – and
die Vereinigten Staaten – the United States
von – from
wie – how
wo – where
woher – where from

Expressions:
Entschuldigung! – Excuse me!; Sorry!
Ich bin müde. – I am tired.
Ich habe Durst. – I am thursty.
Es macht nichts. – Don't worry about it.
Es ist nicht so schlimm. – Don't worry about it.
Natürlich! – Of course!
Natürlich nicht! – Of course not!
Im Gegenteil! – On the contrary!
Sicher! – Certainly!

CHAPTER 4:

aber – but
der/die Angestellte – clerk
die Bäckerei – bakery
höflich – polite
langsam – slow
das Mineralwasser – mineral water
möchten – would like to
Uhr – clock
verstehen – to understand
was – what

Expressions:
Wie viel kostet das? – How much does it cost?
In Ordnung. – OK; All right!
Bitte. – Please.

Bitte schön! – You are welcome.
Vielen Dank. – Thank you very much.
Danke, gern. – Yes, please.
Nein, danke. – No, thanks.
Auf Wiedersehen. – Good bye.

CHAPTER 5:

die Arbeit – work
die Augen – eyes
das Auto – car
beide – both
beschäftigt – busy
die Blume – flower
fahren – to drive
für – for
der Garten – garden
gefallen – to be pleased
die Geschäftsfrau – business woman
groß – big
das Haus – house
klein – small
lustig – funny
manchmal – sometimes
mögen – to like
nach – to
der Programmierer – programmer
sehr – very
der Stern – star
wohnen – to live, to reside
zusammen – together

Die Farben:
rot – red
blau – blue
grün – green
braun – brown
gelb – yellow
schwarz – black
grau – grey
orange – orange
weiß – white
rosa – pink

Die Wochentage:
der Montag – Monday
der Dienstag – Tuesday
der Mittwoch – Wednesday
der Donnerstag – Thursday
der Freitag – Friday
der Samstag – Saturday
der Sonntag – Sunday

Expressions:
ärgerlich werden – to get angry

Es ist mir langweilig. – I am bored.
im Allgemeinen – in general
Liebe auf den ersten Blick – love at first sight

CHAPTER 6:

abbiegen – to turn
die Bank – bank
brauchen – to need
dann – then
die Brücke – bridge
einkaufen – to shop
gegenüber – across
geradeaus – straight ahead
geschlossen – closed
gestern – yesterday
heute – today
hinaufgehen – to go up
hinuntergehen – to go down
das Kaufhaus – department store
das Kino – movie theater
links – left
nahe – close (by)
neben – next to
offen/geöffnet – open
der Park – park
rechts – right
schön – nice
die Straße – street
der Tag – day
überqueren – to cross
ungefähr – about, approximately
weit (weg) – far (away)

Expressions:
Bis später! – See you later!
einkaufen gehen – to go shopping
einen Spaziergang machen – to go for a walk
auf der anderen Seite – on the other side (of)
nach links – to the left
nach rechts – to the right
zu Fuß gehen – to walk

CHAPTER 7:

anschauen – to look at
bleiben – to stay
der Bruder – brother
deshalb – therefore
die Ferien – vacation
ganz – very, all
glücklich – happy
klein – small
lieber – rather

manchmal – sometimes
mögen – to like
der Monat – month
die Mutter – mother
reisen – to travel
die Schwester – sister
Ski laufen – to ski
der Vater – father
verschieden – different
viel – a lot
wandern – to hike

Die Jahreszeit:
der Frühling – spring
der Sommer – summer
der Herbst – autumn
der Winter – winter

Die Monate:
der Januar – January
der Februar – February
der März – March
der April – April
der Mai – May
der Juni – June
der Juli – July
der August – August
der September – September
der Oktober – October
der November – November
der Dezember – December

Expressions:
meiner Meinung nach – in my opinion
in den Bergen – in the mountains
zu Hause – at home
mit anderen Worten – in other words
Ich auch! – Me too!

CHAPTER 8:

besonders – especially
groß – tall, big
gut aussehend – good-looking
die Haare – hair
der Hut – hat
klein – small
kurz – short
lang – tall, long
lebhaft – dynamic, lively
lieben – to love
lustig – funny
nett – nice
tragen – to wear
verheiratet – married

die Ehefrau, die Frau – wife
der Ehemann, der Mann – husband
die Eltern – parents
der Enkel – male grandchild
die Enkelin – female grandchild
die Großmutter – grandmother
der Großvater – grandfather
der Neffe – nephew
die Nichte – niece
der Onkel – uncle
die Schwiegermutter – mother-in-law
der Schwiegervater – father-in-law
der Sohn – son
die Tante – aunt
die Tochter – daughter

Expressions:
mit dem Fahrrad fahren – to ride a bike
Sport treiben – to play a sport, to exercise

CHAPTER 9:

arm – poor
außer – except
bald – soon
der Besuch – visit
furchtbar – terrible
heiß – hot
jeder/e/es – every
kalt – cold
regnen – to rain
der Schnee – snow
schneien – to snow
schwül – humid
sonnig – sunny
vielleicht – maybe
das Wetter – weather
wieder – again
windig – windy

Expressions:
Kopf hoch! – Keep your chin up!
Ich weiß nicht. – I don't know.
Ach du meine Güte! – Oh my goodness!
Schatz – darling

CHAPTER 10:

abfahren – to leave
dasselbe – the same
die Fahrkarten – tickets
das Gleis – track
immer – always
die Minute – minute
unglaublich – unbelievable

die Zeit – time
der Zug – train
der Bahnhof – train station
bekommen – to get

Expressions:
Gute Reise! – Have a nice trip!
Wie viel Uhr ist es? – What time is it?
Mit Vergnügen! – With pleasure!
Das reicht! – That's enough!
Mal sehen … – Let's see …
gute Laune haben – to be in a good mood
schlechte Laune haben – to be in a bad mood
früh sein – to be early
spät sein – to be late
Mist! – Darn!
Wie bitte? – Excuse me?
einfach – one-way
hin und zurück – round-trip

CHAPTER 11:

alt – old
angenehm – comfortable
anstellen – to turn on
der Aufenthaltsraum – family room
besuchen – to visit
das Bett – bed
der Boden – floor
der Computer – computer
der Junge – boy
das Essen – food
das Fenster – window
die Freizeit – freetime
der Herd – stove
der Hund – dog
jung – young
die Katze – cat
kochen – to cook
die Küche – kitchen
der Lärm – noise
leben – to live
lesen – to read
die Leute – people
oft – often
der Papierkorb – wastebasket
riechen – to smell
der Roman – novel
schlafen – to sleep
das Schlafzimmer – bedroom
der Sessel – lounge chair
sitzen – to sit
das Sofa – couch

spielen – to play
die Spielsachen – toys
der Teppich – rug
verstecken – to hide
während – while
weich – soft
das Wohnzimmer – living room
wunderschön – wonderful
ziemlich – quite

in/innen – in, inside
vor – in front of
auf – on
unter – under
hinter – behind
neben – next to
außen/draußen – outside

Expressions:
blitzblank – neat as a pin
ein richtiger Gourmetkoch – a real gourmet cook
bei Tagesanbruch – at the crack of dawn
im oberen Stockwerk – upstairs
im Erdgeschoss – downstairs
Karten spielen – to play cards
es gibt – there is/are
im Internet surfen – to surf the web
Email schicken – to send email

CHAPTER 12:

anrufen – to call (on a phone)
die Besprechung – meeting
das Büro – office
ehrlich – honest
finden – to find
die Firma – company
geben – to give
das Geheimnis – secret
schwimmen – to swim
unterhaltsam – entertaining
warten – to wait
wirklich – really
wissen – to know
das Wochenende – weekend

Expressions:
ein bisschen – a little
Ich muss los. – I'm leaving.
Mir reicht's! – I've had enough!
Es war toll! – It was great!
Tennis spielen – to play tennis
ins Konzert gehen – to go to a concert

Fußball spielen – to play soccer
Basketball spielen – to play basketball
Angst haben – to be afraid
überrascht sein – to be surprised
Du nimmst mich wohl auf den Arm! – You're joking!

CHAPTER 13:

aufwachen – to wake up
der Becher – container, cup
bestellen – to order
die Dose – can
die Flasche – bottle
das Glas – glass
kommen – to come
die Scheibe – slice
sogar – even
das Stück – piece
der Teller – bowl, plate
die Vorspeise – appetizer

die Ananas – pineapple
die Äpfel – apples
die Bananen – bananas
das Bier – beer
das Brot – bread
die Eier – eggs
das Eis – ice cream
die Erbsen – peas
die Erdbeeren – strawberries
der Fisch – fish
das Fleisch – meat
das Gemüse – vegetables
das Getränk – beverage
das Huhn – poultry
der Kaffee – coffee
die Karotten – carrots
der Käse – cheese
die Kirschen – cherries
der Kuchen – cake
der Lachs – salmon
die Milch – milk
der Nachtisch – dessert
das Obst – fruit
die Orangen – oranges
die Pilze – mushrooms
die Pommes Frites – French fries
der Reis – rice
das Rind – beef
der Salat – salad
der Schinken – ham
die Suppe – soup
die Süßigkeiten – candy
der Tee – tea
die Tomaten – tomatoes
die Torte – cake

der Wein – wine
die Zwiebeln – onions

Expressions:
Prost!/Zum Wohl! – Cheers!
Guten Appetit! – Have a good meal!
Sonst noch etwas? – Anything else?
Das hört sich gut an. – That sounds good.
Was für (ein) – What kind of
Ich habe einen Bärenhunger. – I could eat a horse.

CHAPTER 14:

anfangen – to begin
die Erkältung – cold
feiern – to celebrate
fertig – ready
fühlen – to feel
die Gesundheit – health
glauben – to think, to believe
großartig – great
krank – sick
ob – if
der Schmerz – pain
seit – since, for
treffen – to meet
wahrscheinlich – probably
zunehmen – to gain weight

der Arm – arm
das Auge – eye
der Bauch – stomach
das Bein – leg
die Brust – chest
der Ellenbogen – elbow
der Finger – finger
der Fuß – foot
der Hals – neck
die Hand – hand
das Knie – knee
der Kopf – head
der Mund – mouth
die Nase – nose
das Ohr – ear
der Rücken – back
die Schulter – shoulder
der Zahn – tooth
die Zeh – toe

Expressions:
Ich bin erledigt. – I'm exhausted.
Ich habe zu viel zu tun. – I'm swamped.
Ich fühle mich nicht gut. – I don't feel well.
weh tun – to hurt
Herzlichen Glückwunsch zum Geburtstag! – Happy birthday!

CHAPTER 15:

anprobieren – to try (on)
anziehen – to put on
aussehen – to look
furchtbar – terrible
gerade – (just) now
das Geschäft – store
die Größe – size
hübsch – pretty
die Kasse – cash register
die Kleidung – clothing
mitbringen – to bring along
passen – to fit
Recht haben – to be right
die Seide – silk
tragen – to wear
der Urlaub – vacation
zahlen – to pay
der Anzug – suit
die Anzugsjacke – blazer
der Badeanzug – swimsuit
der Bademantel – bathrobe
der Blazer – blazer
die Bluse – blouse
der Büstenhalter – bra
die Fliege – bowtie
die Handschuhe – gloves
die Handtasche – purse
die Hausschuhe – slippers
das Hemd – shirt
die Hose – pants, trousers
der Hut – hat
die Jeans – jeans
das Kleid – dress
die Krawatte – tie
die kurze Hose – shorts
der Mantel – coat
der Pullover – sweater
der Regenmantel – raincoat
der Regenschirm – umbrella
der Rock – skirt
der Schal – scarf
der Schlafanzug – pajama
die Schuhe – shoes
die Socken – socks
die Stiefel – boots
die Strumpfhose – pantyhose
das T-Shirt – T-shirt
die Turnschuhe – tennis shoes
die Unterhose – underpants, slip

Expressions:
Das kommt (gar) nicht in Frage! – No way!
im Angebot – on sale

Das steht dir gut/ausgezeichnet. – That looks great on you.

CHAPTER 16:

anders – different
ankommen – to arrive
der Anrufbeantworter – answering machine
benutzen – to use
der Besitzer – owner
die Besprechung – meeting
der Chef – boss
das Handy – cell phone
der Computer – computer
der Dieb – thief
dort – there
einige – some
endlich – finally
der Erfolg – success
fast – almost
das Feuer – fire
der Flughafen – airport
der Fluss – river
die Geschäftsreise – business trip
das Glück – good luck
die Hilfe – help
hinterlassen – to leave
jemand – somebody
klappen – to work, to function
leider – unfortunately
lesen – to read
mieten – to rent
die Nachricht – message
nämlich – namely
der Notfall – emergency
die Panne – breakdown
passieren – to happen
das Pech – bad luck
der Platten – flat tire
die Polizei – police
schicken – to send
schnell – fast
schreiben – to write
stehlen – to steal
die Tastatur – keyboard
verirren – to get lost
verschütten – to spill
versuchen – to try
zuerst – first

Expressions:
Wie schrecklich! – What a terrible thing!
auf das Land – into the country
Lieber spät als gar nicht! – Better late than never!

GERMANY

GERMAN HISTORY

The calamity of World War II left Europe in ruins and Germany completely destroyed. More than 6 million Jews died under the persecution of the Nazi regime, almost 10 million Germans were killed in the war, and many of the cities were reduced to rubble. Under the governance of the four allied forces, the country was split into French, British, American, and Soviet occupation zones, and the capital city Berlin was divided into four sectors.

The emerging conflict between the Western world and the communist regimes in the East soon shifted attention away from a defeated Germany and focused on the country's strategic position, making Germany the central staging ground of the Cold War. While the United States backed the formation of a democratic government in the Western territories, in the East the Soviet Union promoted regimes in compliance with the communist model.

After France, Great Britain, and the United States had merged the western territories into one region, the Federal Republic of Germany was founded in 1948 with Bonn as its "transitional" capital city. At the same time, East Germany was consolidated into the German Democratic Republic, thus finalizing a process that resulted in the existence of two German states.

The magnitude of the ideological differences and the severity of the Cold War confrontation became apparent in 1961 when the East German government, in an effort to stop the depletion of its population, ordered the construction of a wall through Berlin and began to secure the borders to West Germany. For the next 28 years contact between East and West Germans would be reduced to an absolute minimum and in many cases be entirely impossible, as one of the most fortified borders in history separated families and friends.

With the financial aid of the United States, West Germany soon turned into a thriving industrial state and adapted to the conditions of Western democracy in general. Concurrent with similar developments in postwar society throughout the Western world, Germany experienced a tremendous economic upswing in the 1950s, which brought modern conveniences and prosperity. The late 1960s gave rise to a number of student and youth movements, which critically examined the values of consumer society and lead to a heightened awareness of environmental issues that have become a key theme of all political parties.

As the more moderate policies of the Soviet leader Mikhail Gorbachev relaxed communist control over Eastern Europe in the late 1980s, the unthinkable became reality. On November 9th, 1989 Germans listened in disbelief as the East German government announced the opening of the wall. Thousands of Germans poured out into the streets and embraced each other under the Brandenburg Gate as the world watched. East and West Germany officially united in 1990 and relocated all government offices to Berlin in 2000, ending a period of separation that lasted for almost 50 years.

WHAT ARE THESE GERMANS SAYING?

When foreigners travel through Germany and attempt to utilize some hard-learned German, they will soon find out that communicating in German is one thing, understanding Germans quite another. Comfort may be found in the fact that even a German might be at a loss as to what his fellow German is saying. While standard German is the official language used in schools, universities and throughout the various media, many Germans speak their regional dialects when communicating with family and friends. Dialects are far more than accents and represent different language systems with a unique vocabulary, a distinct pronunciation, and in many cases a divergent grammar structure. Even when Germans speak standard German, the dialect usually colors their speech and reveals their regional origin. The distinctive sound patterns of the different dialects – ranging from modulated singing to guttural explosions – are a source of amusement and are relentlessly exploited by comedians, particularly when politicians are the objects of ridicule. The dominance of the media as the main vehicle of popular culture has raised the concern that dialects might someday become extinct. In an effort to protect dialects, many communities have formed clubs that stage plays performed in the local dialect and sponsor readings of stories and poetry that reflect the local "tongue." Even young Germans have found an interest in dialects, and some rock groups who dye their hair in every color of the rainbow will sing their lyrics in their own dialect accompanied by synthesizer and the electric guitar.

IN LOVE WITH SOCCER

While many different types of sports and athletic activities enjoy great popularity in Germany, soccer is still the unquestioned number one. Every Saturday afternoon between two and four o'clock, thousands of Germans participate in the same ritual. From the half-pint youngster to the beer-bellied family father, whether in a giant stadium or the nearest dirt field – everywhere Germans unite in one common goal: to blast the "round leather" into the opponent's net. When the German National Team plays in a major competition, it is a matter of national importance: Corporate meetings are cut short, university seminars end early, even the Parliament shows suspiciously thinned representation. Police reports showed that the freeways were practically empty when the German team played in the last World Cup championship. Where were the Germans? Glued to their television sets, of course.

JOIN A CLUB

What do Germans do in their free time? They pick a hobby and join a corresponding club. Or they join a local club and find themselves involved in a hobby they never knew existed. Or they invent a hobby and form a new club. Most importantly, they are members of a club, and

there is one for every possible activity under the sun. There are clubs for knitting, sewing, and stitching, for singing and all other forms of using and abusing the human voice such as yodeling, for playing card games, for lovers of model planes and model trains, and for people who build whole architectural models out of matches, for gardeners, beekeepers, and breeders of carrier pigeons, for basket weaving and book binding.

There is even a club whose sole purpose is to maintain and paint local park benches. Many clubs are tightly knit communities where members celebrate their birthday parties, plan trips to local exhibitions or theater performances, and even spend their summer vacations together. While people join to share their passion for a particular hobby with likeminded individuals, the primary purpose of clubs lies in their social function. They provide outsiders and visitors with a platform to gain access to the local community, to socialize, and to make friends.

SHOPPING FRENZY

Considering that the concept of keeping stores open for 24 hours is alien to the German culture, shopping can be a daunting task. Stores usually open between 8 and 9 o'clock in the morning and close around 6 o'clock in the evening. Smaller businesses close for an additional hour during lunch while all stores, including supermarkets and grocery stores, are closed on Saturday afternoons and on Sundays. In addition, many small business owners take Monday off, and certain service industries, such as some restaurants, don't operate on Mondays. Responding to consumer complaints and in an effort to make shopping more flexible and less hectic, the so-called "Long Thursday" was introduced. Keeping stores open until 8 o'clock on Thursday evenings was meant to provide working families with the opportunity to accomplish some of their grocery shopping before the weekend.

The Germans, however, didn't show up. Many small business owners quickly backed out of the arrangement as they were unable to cover their labor costs due to the poor showing of customers.

So when do the Germans shop? Every Saturday morning supermarkets become Darwinian sites where securing a parking spot and hunting down a shopping cart are carefully orchestrated scenarios in which all family members participate. Negotiating overcrowded aisles requires vigilance and planning if the customer intends to avoid being trapped in a sea of shopping carts with no escape in sight. Once the carts are filled to capacity the customer still has to make it past the cash register by enduring a line that can test the patience of even the most unwearied individual.

Finally, when all the shopping bags are stored away in the trunk of the car, a sigh of relief signals that the weekend can officially begin. On Sundays, when the entire country is practically shut down, Germans need to rest from their victorious deeds – until the next weekend.

SIGHTSEEING AND LANDMARKS

Many Americans who travel to Germany are intrigued with the cultural and historical heritage that is visible everywhere. Sites like Schloss Neuschwanstein, built by Ludwig II at the end of the 19th century and the inspiration for Disneyland, the town of Oberammergau with its famous Passion Play originating in 1634, and the vacation resort of Garmisch-Partenkirchen, all draw thousands of tourists every year to the region of Southern Bavaria.

In the West, the many castles towering upon the cliffs along the Rhine give evidence of a time when knights were in command of shipping and trading on the river. Smaller towns like Heidelberg, Freiburg, Tübingen, Marburg, Göttingen, and Münster have retained many of their medieval features. Narrow cobblestone streets lined by tilted houses that seem to lean on each other create a picturesque scene that invites the visitor to make a stop in one of the many street cafes and beer gardens.

Along with the reunification came new travel opportunities into the eastern part of Germany. The city of Dresden with its magnificent baroque and rococo architecture impresses the visitor.

The Zwinger Palace accommodates some of the most famed museums in Europe including an exhibition of early Meissen china and the Semper Gallery housing Raphael's Sistine Madonna.

And then there is Berlin, the cultural capital of Germany since the 17th century. As the capital of Prussia, then the German Empire under Wilhelm I, and throughout the Weimar Republic and the Third Reich, German history in all of its high and low points is discernible at every turn.

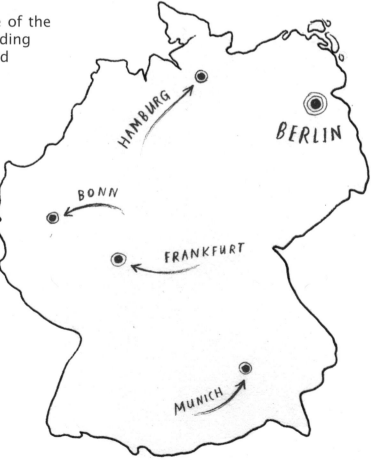

(es ist meer egaal)
Es ist mir egal.
I don't care.

1

(lahs u'ns gé-en)
Lass uns gehen.
Let's go

2

(der mahn)
der Mann
man

3

(gooten mo'rgen)
Guten Morgen!
Good morning!

4

(dee frou)
die Frau
woman

5

(esen)
essen
to eat

6

(frühSCHtüken)
frühstücken
To have breakfast

7

(iCH hahbe hu'nger)
Ich habe Hunger!
I'm hungry!

8

10

9

12

11

14

13

16

15

(glükliCH)
glücklich
happy

9

(trourig)
traurig
sad

10

(froyndinen)
Freundinnen
friends (female form)

11

(kaze)
käse
cheese

12

(gében)
gében
give

13

(iCH haabe doorst)
Ich habe Durst
I'm thirsty

14

(iCH bin müde)
Ich bin müde
I'm tired.

15

(es mahCHt niCHts)
Es macht nichts
Don't worry about it.

16

95626-00

18

17

20

19

22

21

24

23

(po'stkahrten)
Postkarten
postcards

17

(breefmahrken)
Briefmarken
stamps

18

(kahrten)
Karten.
tickets

19

(tahssen kahfé)
Tassen Kaffee.
cups of coffee

20

(SCHtifte)
stifte.
pens

21

(es ist mir lahngvayliCH)
Es ist mir langweilig.
I am bored

22

(angerliCH verden)
argerlich warden
to get angry

23

(hous)
das Haus
house

24

26

25

28

27

30

29

32

31

(outO)
das Auto
car

25

(der SCHtern)
der Stern
star

26

(ouf der ahnderen sayte)
auf der anderen Seite
on the other side (of)

27

(gegenüber)
gegenuber
facing

28

(NahCH links)
nach links
to the left

29

(geradeous)
geradeaus
straight ahead

30

(nahCH reCHts)
nach rechts
to the right

31

(der hoot)
der Hut
Hat

32

34

33

36

35

38

37

40

39

(der é-e-mun)
der Ehemann
husband

(dee-é-e-frou)
die Ehefrau
wife

33

(VindiCH)
Es ist windig
It's windy

34

(regnet)
Es regnet.
It's raining

35

(zo'nig)
Es ist sonnig.
It's sunny

36

(SCHnayt)
Es schneit.
It's snowing.

37

(früh sayn)
früh sein.
to be early.

38

(SCHpat sayn)
spät sein.
to be late.

39

(blitzblahnk)
blitzblank
neat as a pin

40

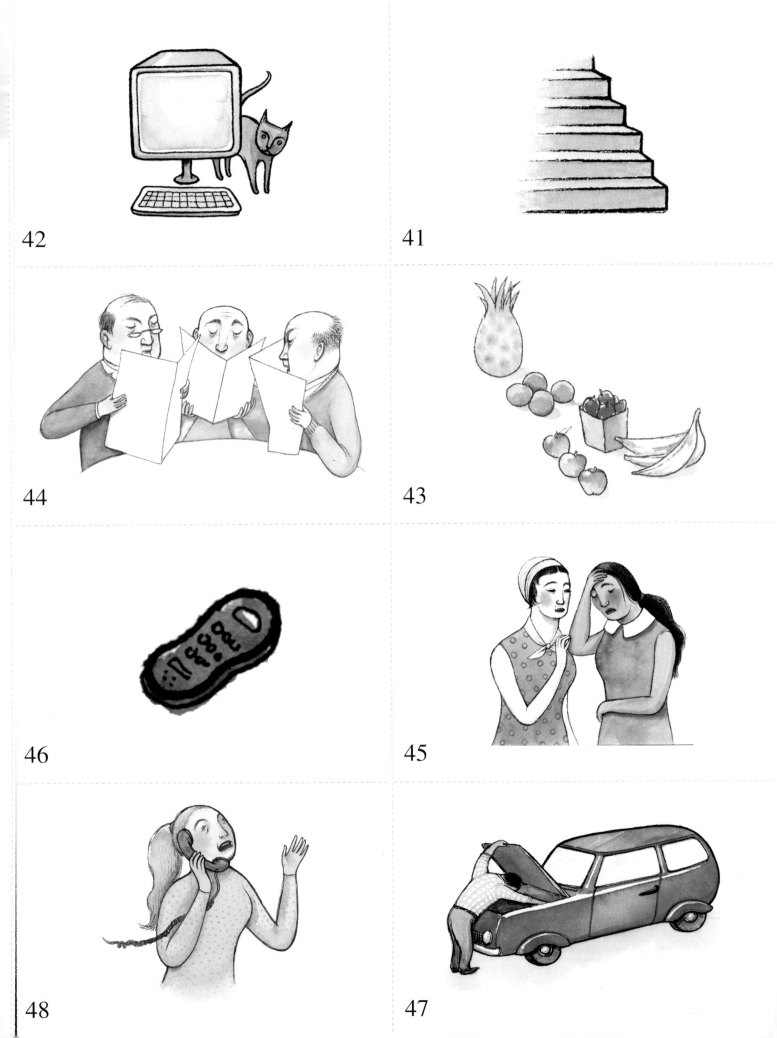

42

41

44

43

46

45

48

47

(im Oberen SCHto'kverk)
im oberen Stockwerk
upstairs

41

(der kompYooter)
der Computer
computer

42

(opst)
das Obst
fruit

43

bestellen
order

44

(füle)
Ich fühle mich nicht gut.
I don't feel well.

45

(handi)
das Handy
cell phone

46

(pahne)
panne
breakdown

47

Rufen Sie die Feuerwehr an!
Call the fire department!

48

(es ist meer egaal)
Es ist mir egal.
I don't care.

(gooten mo'rgen)
Guten Morgen!
Good morning!

(moCHten)
möchten
would like

Ich nehme den Zug.
I'm taking the train.

(ferlast)
verlässt
leave

(iCH hayse)
Ich heiße...
my name is...

Woher kommen Sie?
Where are you from?

Ich habe Durst.
I have thirst.

(feelen dahnk)
Vielen Dank.
Thank you very much.

(nayn dahnke)
Nein, danke.
No, thank you.

(dee SCHtraase)
die Straße
street

(vOhin)
Wohin gehst du?
Where are you going?

(flooghaafen)
Flughafen
airport

(vee ist dahs vetter)
Wie ist das Wetter?
What's the weather?

(kahlt)
Es ist kalt.
It's cold.

(vee feel oor ist es)
Wie viel Uhr ist es?
Do you have the time?

(lahs u'ns gé-en)
Lass uns gehen.
Let's go.

(vee get es deer)
Wie geht es dir?
How are you?

(dahs aabentessen)
das Abendessen
dinner

(iCH hahbe hu'nger)
Ich habe Hunger!
I'm hungry!

(entSCHu'ldigu'ng)
Entschuldigung.
Excuse me.

Wie alt bist du?
How old are you?

Wie heißt du?
What's your name?

Ich habe Hunger.
I have hunger.

(ouf veedersén)
Auf Wiedersehen!
Good bye!

(dahnke gern)
Danke, gern!
Yes, please!

(dee brüke)
die Brücke
bridge

(velCHe yaareszayt hahst doo leeber)
Welche Jahreszeit hast du lieber?
Which season do you prefer?

(dahs ist mayne fumeelee-e)
Das ist meine Familie.
This is my family.

(hays)
Es ist heiß.
It's hot.

Verstehen Sie das?
Do you understand?

(vahs moCHtest doo essen)
Was möchtest du essen?
What do you want to eat?